THE TERRIBLE
SPEED OF MERCY

THE TERRIBLE SPEED OF MERCY

A Spiritual Biography of Flannery O'Connor

JONATHAN ROGERS

THOMAS NELSON
Since 1798

NASHVILLE   DALLAS   MEXICO CITY   RIO DE JANEIRO

Published in Nashville, Tennessee, by Thomas Nelson. Thomas Nelson is a registered trademark of Thomas Nelson, Inc.

Published in association with Eames Literary Services, LLC, Nashville, Tennessee.

Thomas Nelson, Inc., titles may be purchased in bulk for educational, business, fund-raising, or sales promotional use. For information, please e-mail SpecialMarkets@ThomasNelson.com.

Library of Congress Cataloging-in-Publication Data

Rogers, Jonathan, 1969-
 The terrible speed of mercy : a spiritual biography of Flannery O'Connor / Jonathan Rogers.
   p. cm.
 Includes bibliographical references.
 ISBN 978-1-59555-023-1
 1. O'Connor, Flannery. 2. Authors, American--20th century--Biography. I. Title.
 PS3565.C57Z853 2012
 813'.54--dc23
 [B]

2011052998

Printed in the United States of America

12 13 14 15 16 QG 6 5 4 3 2 1

To Andrew Peterson

and the rest of the Rabbit Room community

PUBLISHER'S NOTE

A highly offensive racial slur occurs some thirteen times throughout this book, in each case quoted from Flannery O'Connor's
fiction or correspondence. The publishing team discussed at
some length how best to handle this word in light of the sensibilities of twenty-first century readers. In the end, we decided
to let the word stand in its full offensiveness, on the grounds
that the repugnance the reader feels at the word is a key reason
O'Connor used it in the first place. It may be true that there was
more open racism in the 1950s and 1960s than in the twenty-
first century, but that hardly explains why O'Connor used the
"n-word" in the thirteen instances quoted in this book. A reader
of literary fiction in the 1950s would be no less offended by
the word than a reader of literary fiction in 2012. To expurgate
O'Connor's language would be to suggest that we understand its
offensiveness better than she does, or perhaps to suggest that the
readers of this book are more easily offended than O'Connor's
original audience. We have no reason to believe that either is true.
So we leave O'Connor's language intact, and we leave you with
this warning: you may find some of the language in this book
offensive; that is as it should be.

CONTENTS

INTRODUCTION

Flannery O'Connor was twenty-seven years old when her debut novel *Wise Blood* was published. She was small of frame and sweet-faced in spite of the fact that she had already lived for two years with lupus. She was mostly quiet in public, but when she did speak she spoke in the lilting tones of Georgia's Piedmont. She did not, in short, come across as a force to be reckoned with.

While visiting friends in Nashville, O'Connor encountered a man who put into words what many of the people who met her must have been thinking about the young author of *Wise Blood*. "That was a profound book," he said. "You don't look like you wrote it."

O'Connor described the scene in a letter to Elizabeth and Robert Lowell. She wrote, "I mustered up my squintiest expression and snarled, 'Well I did.'"[1]

She did indeed. She who lived a comfortable, conventional, pious middle-class existence on a dairy farm in Milledgeville, Georgia, wrote stories that are like literary thunderstorms, turning on sudden violence and flashes of revelation that crash down from the heavens, destroying even as they illuminate.

Nothing about O'Connor's outward demeanor would suggest that such storms surged within her. Hers was a quiet life—not free from trouble by any means, but regular and stable. Except for five and a half years in her early twenties—years spent training as a writer in Iowa, New York, and Connecticut—she spent her whole life in Georgia, under her mother's roof. Her mother could be domineering, but she was solicitous of Flannery's health and well-being, and she always gave her daughter the space to do her work, even if she didn't always appreciate the work she was doing.

Flannery O'Connor and her mother lived a most regulated, most devout life on the farm they called Andalusia. They rose every morning for six o'clock prayers, then rode together to Sacred Heart Catholic Church for seven o'clock Mass. They sat in the same pew every day.

After Mass, the O'Connor women returned to the farmhouse, and Flannery sat down at the typewriter in the front room that used to be the parlor. There—every morning including Sundays—she spent four hours writing stories about street preachers, prostitutes, juvenile delinquents, backwater prophets, hardscrabble farmers, sideshow freaks, murderers, charlatans, and amputees while her mother tended to the business of the house and farm.

Then, at noon, the O'Connor women drove back into town, where they had lunch at the Sanford House tearoom among the hatted and white-gloved ladies of Milledgeville's patrician class. Flannery was especially fond, according to biographer Brad Gooch, of the fried shrimp at Sanford House and the peppermint chiffon pie.

No, Flannery O'Connor didn't look like she could have written *Wise Blood* or *The Violent Bear It Away* or "A Good Man Is

Hard to Find." Nothing about her life story seems to account for the particular genius—the seedy, violent, white-trash genius—that defines her fiction. "There won't be any biographies written of me," she wrote, "because, for only one reason, lives spent between the house and the chicken yard do not make exciting copy."[2] Her life wasn't as uneventful as all that. Scholars including Jean Cash, Paul Elie, and Brad Gooch have demonstrated that her life did indeed provide the raw material for a fascinating biography. It is true, however, that her life was mostly free of the drama and self-indulgence and entanglements that often make for more "exciting copy" in her peers' biographies. There were no blowups or meltdowns or crack-ups or addictions in Flannery O'Connor's life. There was mostly a quiet attention to the work at hand.

Flannery O'Connor wrote of the great mysteries. She wrote *in* the great mysteries and was a mystery herself. In "The Life You Save May Be Your Own," Mr. Shiftlet speaks to the mysteries of the human heart in his first meeting with Lucynell Crater.

> "Lady," he said, and turned and gave her his full attention, "lemme tell you something. There's one of them doctors in Atlanta that's taken a knife and cut the human heart—the human heart," he repeated, leaning forward, "out of a man's chest and held it in his hand," and he held his hand out, palm up, as if it were slightly weighted with the human heart, "and studied it like it was a day-old chicken, and lady," he said, allowing a long significant pause in which his head slid forward and his clay-colored eyes brightened, "he don't know no more about it than you or me."
>
> "That's right," the old woman said.
>
> "Why, if he was to take that knife and cut into every corner

of it, he still wouldn't know no more about it than you or me. What you want to bet?"

"Nothing," the old woman said wisely.[3]

The biographer of Flannery O'Connor is in the same fix as that doctor in Atlanta. No amount of poking around in the external events and facts of her life is going to get at the heart of her. There's no accounting for Flannery O'Connor in those terms. Thankfully we have her letters, which provide windows into an inner life where whole worlds orbited and collided.

The outward constraints that O'Connor accepted and ultimately cultivated made room for an interior world as spacious and various as the heavens themselves. Her natural curiosity was harnessed and directed by an astonishing intellectual and spiritual rigor. She read voraciously, from the ancients to contemporary Catholic theologians to periodicals to novels. She once referred to herself as a "hillbilly Thomist."[4] She was joking, but the phrase turns out to be helpful. The raw material of her fiction was the lowest common denominator of American culture, but the sensibility that shaped the hillbilly raw material into art shared more in common with Thomas Aquinas and the other great minds of the Catholic tradition than with any practitioner of American letters, high or low.

In a letter to editor John Selby, O'Connor spoke of "the peculiarity or aloneness, if you will, of the experience I write from."[5] She didn't write this letter from the farm in Milledgeville. She wrote from the storied Yaddo artists' colony, where she was working alongside such literary lights as Robert Lowell and Malcolm Cowley. She was fresh off three years at the Iowa Writers' Workshop, then as now one of the most respected MFA programs in the country. Tastemakers in the literary establishment—not all of them, but plenty of them—welcomed her and recognized her as one of the great talents. When she wrote of her aloneness, she was writing from a place very near the epicenter of American letters. From very early in her career, she jealously guarded her aloneness, her peculiarity, for her peculiarity was the peculiarity of a prophet. Her voice was the voice of one crying in the wilderness.

Perhaps the surest measure of O'Connor's sense of calling was her willingness to be misunderstood. She didn't expect the literary establishment to understand what she was up to. Nor was she especially bothered when her coreligionists misunderstood her—which was just as well, for almost all of the Christians who knew her work misunderstood it. A "real ugly" letter from a woman in Boston was typical: "She said she was a Catholic and so she couldn't understand how anybody could even HAVE such thoughts."[6]

O'Connor made it clear in her letters and essays, however, that she wrote such shocking fiction not in spite of her Christian faith, but because of it. "It is when the individual's faith is weak, not when it is strong, that he will be afraid of an honest fictional representation of life,"[7] she wrote. Flannery O'Connor wrote what she saw, and she saw a world that was broken beyond self-help or "Instant Uplift"—but a world also in which transcendence was forever threatening to break through, welcome or not. O'Connor's opponents, therefore, included not only the religious skeptic, but also the religious believer who thinks that "the eyes of the Church or of the Bible or of his particular theology have already done the seeing for him."[8]

O'Connor's challenge, her calling, was to offer up the truths of the faith to a world that, to her way of thinking, had mostly lost its ability to see and hear such truths.

When you can assume that your audience holds the same beliefs you do you can relax a little and use more normal means of talking to it; when you have to assume that it does not, then you have to make your vision apparent by shock—to the hard of hearing you shout, and for the almost-blind you draw large and startling figures.[9]

To smugness and self-reliance and self-satisfaction in all its forms—from pseudointellectualism to pharisaism to fundamentalism to the false gospel of postwar optimism, with its positive thinking gurus and its can-do advice columnists and its faith in modern science—O'Connor's fiction shouts, "Thus saith the Lord!"

The violence, the sudden death, the ugliness in O'Connor's fiction are large figures drawn for the almost-blind. If the stories offend conventional morality, it is because the gospel itself is an offense to conventional morality. Grace is a scandal; it always has been. Jesus put out the glad hand to lepers and cripples and prostitutes and losers of every stripe even as he called the self-righteous a brood of vipers.

In "A Good Man Is Hard to Find," it is painful to see a mostly harmless old grandmother come to terms with God and herself only at gunpoint. It is even more painful to see her get shot anyway. In a more properly moral story, she would be rewarded for her late-breaking insight and her life would be spared. But the story only enacts what Christians say they believe already: that to lose one's body for the sake of one's soul is a good trade indeed. It's a mystery, and no small part of the mystery is the reader's visceral reaction to truths he or she claims to believe already. O'Connor invites us to step into such mysteries, but she never resolves them. She never reduces them to something manageable.

O'Connor speaks with the ardor of an Old Testament prophet

in her stories. She's like an Isaiah who never quite gets around to "Comfort ye my people." Except for this: there is a kind of comfort in finally facing the truth about oneself. That's what happens in every one of Flannery O'Connor's stories: in a moment of extremity, a character—usually a self-satisfied, self-sufficient character—finally comes to see the truth of his situation. He is accountable to a great God who is the source of all. He inhabits mysteries that are too great for him. And for the first time there is hope, even if he doesn't understand it yet.

Truth is hard for O'Connor's characters; she seems to take it as a point of honor not to make truth easy for the reader either. But there is at least one moment in which she pulls back the veil and gives the reader a more direct glimpse of what she's really up to with all the freakishness and ugliness in her fiction. The main character of the story "Revelation" is the outlandishly smug Ruby Turpin, a small landowner who spends her quiet moments reflecting on how thankful she is to be exactly who and what she is, and not black or white trash or ugly or ungrateful. Her self-satisfied reflections in a doctor's waiting room are interrupted by a girl—a perfect stranger—who hits her in the head with a textbook and chokes her. The girl locks eyes with Mrs. Turpin and says, "Go back to hell where you came from, you old warthog."[10]

Mrs. Turpin takes the girl's words as a message from God, and she takes God to task for it. After all she's done, she believes, she deserves better treatment from the Almighty. There was a whole family of white trash in that waiting room, yet it was Ruby Turpin who was singled out. "What do you send me a message like that for?" she demands. "How am I a hog and me both? How am I saved and from hell too? . . . If you like trash better, go get yourself some trash. Or a nigger. If trash is what you wanted why didn't you make me trash?"[11]

It is perhaps the first honest question Mrs. Turpin has ever asked, and God gives her an answer. The setting sun has left one purple streak in the sky; as Mrs. Turpin gazes at the streak, her earthly sight gives way to a heavenly vision:

> She saw the streak as a vast swinging bridge extending upward from the earth through a field of living fire. Upon it a vast horde of souls were rumbling toward heaven. There were whole companies of white-trash, clean for the first time in their lives, and bands of black niggers in white robes, and battalions of freaks and lunatics shouting and clapping and leaping like frogs. And bringing up the end of the procession was a tribe of people whom she recognized at once as those who, like her and Claud, had always had a little of everything and the God-given wit to use it right. . . . They alone were on key. Yet she could see by their shocked and altered faces that even their virtues were being burned away. [12]

Blessed are the freaks and the lunatics, who at least have sense enough not to put any faith in their own respectability or virtue or talents. The freaks in O'Connor's stories stand for all of us, deformed in so many ways by original sin. All of us, as the old hymn says, are "weak and wounded, sick and sore . . . lost and ruined by the fall." [13] The freakishness and violence in O'Connor's stories, so often mistaken for a kind of misanthropy, turn out to be a call to mercy.

In O'Connor's unique vision, the physical world, even at its seediest and ugliest, is a place where grace still does its work. In fact, it is *exactly* the place where grace does its work. Truth tells itself here, no matter how loud it has to shout.

1 | THE GIRL WHO FOUGHT WITH ANGELS: SAVANNAH, 1925–1939

"Anybody who has survived his childhood," wrote Flannery O'Connor, "has enough information about life to last him the rest of his days."[1] Her childhood began in Savannah, Georgia, on March 25, 1925. O'Connor was born in St. Joseph's, a Catholic hospital of which her family were important benefactors, and she was brought home to Lafayette Square, the very center of Catholic culture in Savannah. Across the square from her tall, narrow row house was St. John's Cathedral, built in part through the generosity of John Flannery, the relative for whom Flannery O'Connor was named. At one corner of the square was the St. Vincent's Grammar School for Girls. At the opposite corner was the Marist Brothers School for Boys. Though Savannah (like the rest of the American South) was overwhelmingly Protestant, Flannery O'Connor's neighbors on Lafayette Square and adjacent streets were mostly Catholic.

O'Connor's family was Irish Catholic on both sides. Flannery's great-grandfather Patrick O'Connor came from Ireland to Savannah in 1851, along with his brother Daniel. Patrick O'Connor opened a livery stable on Broughton Street, about a half mile from Lafayette Square. Patrick's son, Edward Francis O'Connor, was a wholesaler of candies and tobacco and a banker in Savannah. His son, Edward Francis Jr., was Flannery O'Connor's father.

On her mother's side, Flannery's roots went even deeper into the Georgia soil. Her ancestors, Treanors and Hartys, first arrived in Taliaferro County, Georgia—about fifty miles northeast of Milledgeville—with a group of Irish Catholic families who emigrated from Maryland late in the eighteenth century. By 1845, Hugh Treanor, Flannery's great-grandfather, had come to Milledgeville, which was the capital of Georgia at the time. There he owned a gristmill powered by the Oconee River. The first Mass said in Milledgeville, according to Flannery O'Connor, was said in her great-grandfather's hotel room.

Two of Hugh Treanor's daughters married Peter J. Cline successively. Cline was a wealthy merchant and farmer; later in life he was the mayor of Milledgeville. Though Catholic, the Clines were among the most prominent families in Protestant Milledgeville. Cline fathered sixteen children with his two Treanor wives, one of whom was Regina Cline, Flannery O'Connor's mother.

Regina Cline met Edward O'Connor in 1922 when her brother married Edward's sister. The handsome World War I veteran was a little below Regina's social station. But at twenty-six (the same age as Edward) Regina may have felt a certain urgency to find a husband. On October 14, 1922, less than three months after they met, the couple was married.

A few months after the wedding, Regina's cousin Katie

Semmes gave the O'Connors a loan that allowed them to move into the row house she owned on Lafayette Square. In a family full of strong and independent women, Cousin Katie was a towering figure. In her early fifties at the time, she was the widow of Raphael Semmes, nephew of the celebrated confederate admiral of the same name. She was also very wealthy; her father John Flannery, a banker and cotton merchant, left her nearly a million dollars when he died. Cousin Katie was generous with her money. Besides bankrolling her cousin's living arrangements, she had funded the Flannery Memorial Wing at St. Joseph's Hospital, a few blocks from her house. When Regina O'Connor gave birth to a daughter in that very hospital, she named the girl Mary Flannery in honor of the cousin who had been so generous to her and Edward.

For all her generosity, however, Cousin Katie could be controlling. When she bought and moved into the row house next door to the O'Connors, she cast an even longer shadow. She actually bought two houses on Lafayette Square besides the one where the O'Connors lived. She tore one of them down in order to have a place to park her electric car.

With Edward O'Connor's real estate business struggling, the O'Connors took care to cultivate Cousin Katie's goodwill. Biographer Jean Cash reports a revealing anecdote from a conversation she had with Sister Consolata, one of Mary Flannery's teachers at St. Vincent's: "I used to call her Mary O'Connor," said Sister Consolata. "And the mother came and she said, 'Sister, please, whatever you do, you can drop the Mary, but be sure to call her Flannery because of the income.'"[2]

The little girl was known as Mary Flannery throughout her childhood and until she moved away to Iowa for graduate school. Her family and family friends called her Mary Flannery for the whole of her life. Mary Flannery was an unusual child, though not in a Wednesday Addams way, as readers of her grotesque stories might imagine. An only child, she spent almost all her time with adults. From her earliest years she spoke to adults as if they were peers.[3] She always called her parents by their first names.

Mary Flannery's parents doted on their intelligent daughter and were highly protective of her. When she started school at St. Vincent's, on the other side of their quiet square, Regina walked with her every day rather than letting her walk with her classmates, who mostly made their way by themselves. Mary Flannery walked back across the square to eat lunch at home rather than eating with the other girls, until the nuns changed the rules and made her eat at school. Then she brought castor oil sandwiches so her classmates would not ask her to join in on their lunch-trading.

Mary Flannery was not especially well-liked by her peers; the feeling was mutual. When Regina made her take ballet lessons, her physical awkwardness became a metaphor for her social awkwardness. Looking back on the episode from adulthood, O'Connor wrote:

> I was, in my early days, forced to take dancing to throw me into the company of other children and to make me graceful. Nothing I hated worse than the company of other children and I vowed I'd see them all in hell before I would make the first graceful move.[4]

Elsewhere O'Connor described her youthful self as "a pidgeon-toed, only-child with a receding chin and a you-leave-me-alone-or-I'll-bite-you complex."[5]

Most of Mary Flannery's playtime with other children was arranged and scheduled by Regina and often consisted of Mary

Flannery setting her friends down and making them listen to her read stories that she had written. A cousin recalled little Mary Flannery tying one of her friends to a chair. One childhood friend described her not as misanthropic so much as afflicted by a loneliness that was exacerbated by the fact that she simply did not know how to make friends. And her mother, it seems, gave her little opportunity to figure it out for herself. Regina had a list of the children who were allowed to play with her daughter, and she was serious about it. A friend once came to the O'Connors' to play—at Regina's invitation—but she made the mistake of bringing a friend who hadn't been invited. Regina sent both girls home forthwith.[6]

What Mary Flannery couldn't get from her peers, she tried to get from the chickens and ducks that she raised in the tiny backyard of the house on Lafayette Square. According to O'Connor, her obsession with chickens grew out of her first brush with fame. Somehow the people at Pathé News—makers of newsreels for movie theaters—found out about one of her chickens that could walk backward. They sent a cameraman from New York to Savannah to get footage of the unusual chicken and its five-year-old owner.

"From that day with the Pathé man I began to collect chickens," she wrote.

> What had been only a mild interest became a passion, a quest. I had to have more and more chickens. I favored those with one green eye and one orange or with overlong necks and crooked combs. I wanted one with three legs or three wings, but nothing in that line turned up. . . . I could sew in a fashion and I began to make clothes for chickens. A gray bantam named Colonel Eggbert wore a whte pique coat with a lace collar and two buttons in the back.[7]

Her taste for the ridiculous—and her interest in the grotesque—started early, it seems. O'Connor wrote her school
papers about chickens and ducks whether chickens or ducks
were appropriate to the assignment or not; and they usually
were not. When she took home economics in high school, she
made clothes for a duck. She drew pictures of chickens ("beginning at the tail, the same chicken over and over") and wrote
stories about geese. Barnyard fowl would be a lifelong hobby of
O'Connor's, culminating with the peafowl that came to be her
trademark.

When she was not with her ducks and chickens, Mary
Flannery was often drawing and writing. She typed and bound
several copies of a booklet entitled "My Relitives," in which she
described, in satirical tones, several members of her family. Brad
Gooch wrote, "The series of portraits was so finely drawn and
uncomfortably close to life, that the relatives given this treatment . . . either hesitated—or simply refused—to recognize
themselves." O'Connor wrote to her friend Maryat Lee of the
work, "it was not well received."[8]

Cartooning was another interest of Mary Flannery's that
would find expression later in life. Kathleen Feeley described a
cartoon from O'Connor's youth that is revealing in more ways
than one. The cartoon, labeled "age 9," depicts Regina, Edward,
and Mary Flannery O'Connor. The mother says, "Hold your
head up, Mary Flannery, and you are just as bad, Ed." The little
girl says, "I was readin where somebody died of holding up
their head."[9] The overbearing mother bosses both the daughter
and the father. The daughter sasses back; the father is silent,
neither taking up for himself nor correcting his daughter. The
one-panel concision with which the nine-year-old O'Connor
captured the family dynamic is astonishing. Her use of the

telling detail to tell a whole history would be one of the trademarks of her adult fiction.

O'Connor also read voraciously as a child, though by her own account, her reading was not always the most edifying. She read the Greek and Roman myths from a children's encyclopedia, but she also confessed that she read less edifying works:

> The rest of what I read was Slop with a capital S. The Slop period was followed by the Edgar Allan Poe period which lasted for years and consisted chiefly in a volume called *The Humerous Tales of E.A. Poe*. These were mighty humerous—one about a young man who was too vain to wear his glasses and consequently married his grandmother by accident; another about a fine figure of a man who in his room removed wooden arms, wooden legs, hair piece, artificial teeth, voice box, etc. etc.; another about the inmates of a lunatic asylum who take over the establishment and run it to suit themselves. This is an influence I would rather not think about.[10]

If O'Connor herself preferred not to think about Poe's influence, it is understandable, but it is hard for the reader not to delight in the thought of those funny, macabre stories of wooden legs and insane asylums going into young Mary Flannery's imagination and coming out again decades later in the grotesque stories of her adult career.

The O'Connors were a devout family, attending Mass together every day. "I am a born Catholic," Flannery O'Connor wrote to a friend, "went to Catholic schools in my early years, and have never left or wanted to leave the Church."[11] Nevertheless, the O'Connors also instilled in their daughter a certain independence when it came to matters they judged not to be of theological importance—particularly the rules laid down by the nuns at St. Vincent's. Perhaps it came of the fact that Regina's family had been such important benefactors of the Catholic institutions of Savannah and Milledgeville, but the O'Connors expected some latitude when it came to the rules that their co-parishioners followed. Mary Flannery, for instance, skipped the mandatory children's Mass at St. John's Cathedral every Sunday, instead attending Mass with her parents. Each Monday morning the nuns at St. Vincent's checked the previous day's attendance record to see if their students had attended children's Mass, and every Sunday Mary Flannery had not. A classmate reminisced, "She'd stand there and tell sister, 'The Catholic Church does not dictate to my family what time I go to Mass.'"[12] She was six years old when she made this declaration.

O'Connor's relation to religious authority was always complex. On matters of ultimate importance, she submitted unequivocally to the teaching of the church. She welcomed dogma, describing it as "the guardian of mystery." In the face of the great mysteries, she rested in the doctrines of the church, confident that she did not have to grasp a thing in order to believe it.

On the other hand, O'Connor had little patience for sentimentalized versions of the faith, even if they came from those who were in authority over her. She spoke disparagingly of "baby stories and nun stories and young girl stories—a nice vapid-Catholic distrust of finding God in action of any range and depth."[13] If the church that nurtured O'Connor from the cradle caused her distress ("It seems to be a fact that you have to suffer as much from the Church as for it," she wrote), it was because she could never imagine finding real meaning anywhere else. She wrote, "I think that the Church is the only thing that is going to make the terrible world we are coming to endurable; the only thing that makes the Church endurable is that it is somehow the body of Christ and that on this we are fed."[14]

The tortured artist battling his inner demons is a time-honored cliché. Flannery O'Connor was more likely to battle her angels. When she was a student at St. Vincent's she often heard from the Sisters that she had a guardian angel who never left her side. The idea was not altogether comforting to young Mary Flannery:

> I developed something the Freudians have not named—anti-angel aggression, call it. From 8 to 12 years it was my habit to seclude myself in a locked room every so often and with a fierce (and evil) face, whirl around in a circle with my fists knotted, socking the angel. . . . My dislike of him was poisonous. I'm sure I even kicked at him and landed on the floor. You couldn't hurt an angel but I would have been happy to know I had dirtied his feathers.[15]

O'Connor's fiction has been described as having an Old Testament flavor insofar as "the character's relation is directly with God rather than with other people."[16] The same might be said of the lonely little girl flailing away at her guardian angel. There is an Old Testament passion, even ferocity about it. She believed in the angel not because it was "emotionally satisfying"[17] to do so, but because she had it on good authority that he was real. For all her rage and terror, disbelief seems never to have occurred to her any more than a rebellious child might disbelieve in her parents. Jacob, too, fought with an angel, hanging on for dear life until he got both a blessing and a wound that left him limping for the rest of his life.

⁂

At the beginning of Mary Flannery's sixth-grade year, Regina rather abruptly pulled her out of the neighborhood school and put her in Sacred Heart School. Sacred Heart was only a mile distant, but it belonged to another parish. Leaving St. Vincent's was an unusual move for parishioners as faithful as the O'Connors, and it caused a "minor scandal" among the neighbors, who speculated about their reasons for sending their daughter to the tonier school down Abercorn Street.[18]

The move to Sacred Heart was the first of several big changes that Mary Flannery would experience over the next couple of years. She was entering a time of life, of course, when everything changes. But having been a grown-up all her life in some ways, in other ways she held tenaciously to her childhood, resisting the inward changes that other girls experienced with dawning puberty. "When I was twelve I made up my mind absolutely that I would not get any older," she wrote when she was twenty-nine.

> I don't remember how I meant to stop it. There was something about "teen" attached to anything that was repulsive to me. I certainly didn't approve of what I saw of people that age. I was a very ancient twelve; my views at that age would have done credit to a Civil War veteran. I am much younger now than I was at twelve or anyway, less burdened. The weight of centuries lies on children, I'm sure of it.[19]

It was 1937—the year Mary Flannery turned twelve—when her father showed the first visible signs of lupus, the autoimmune disease that would kill him four years later. The same disease would kill Flannery O'Connor at the age of thirty-nine. At that early stage, when the first skin discolorations began to show on Edward's face, the family apparently did not discuss his disease openly. But Mary Flannery was an observant girl, and she must have known something was wrong. In the late 1930s, there was no real treatment for lupus, as there would be when Flannery herself contracted the disease in 1950. The victim simply suffered until he or she died, the immune system eroding various bodily systems. The patient was subject to almost any combination of aches and pains and fevers. And fatigue, there was always fatigue. Childhood friends of Mary Flannery who remembered little else about Edward O'Connor remembered that he regularly took naps after lunch.[20]

Even in the Roaring Twenties, and despite the financial backing of Cousin Katie, Edward O'Connor's real estate business never took off. Not surprisingly, things weren't any better during the Depression years. He enjoyed considerably more success in the less remunerative realm of veterans' affairs; in 1936 he was elected commander of the American Legion for the state of Georgia. The Legion was the one area of his life that was not dominated by his wife and the women of her extended family.

By the end of 1937 Edward O'Connor was looking to parlay family connections (his wife's family, not his own) into government work and more regular pay than real estate had provided. In 1938 his efforts paid off. He took a job in Atlanta as an appraiser for the Federal Housing Authority.

The O'Connors left Savannah in the spring of 1938. They never lived there again. Regina and Mary Flannery moved into the Cline mansion in Milledgeville with Regina's unmarried older sisters, Mary Cline (often called "Sister") and Katie Cline. Mary played the role of matriarch in Milledgeville in much the same way Katie Semmes had played that role in Savannah.

Edward O'Connor spent weeknights in Atlanta. On weekends he made the hundred-mile drive to Milledgeville to be with his wife and daughter and sisters-in-law. A weekend visitor to the Clines' family seat, he was less relevant than ever to the everyday life of the family.

In 1939, Regina and Mary Flannery moved to Atlanta to live with Edward in a house in the Buckhead neighborhood. Mary Flannery attended the new North Fulton High School for the 1939–1940 school year. But by the time the next school year began, she and her mother were back in Milledgeville with the aunts; Edward stayed on with two of Regina's brothers in a boardinghouse known as Bell House.

That fall, Edward's precarious health began to deteriorate. He was forced to quit his job in Atlanta and move to Milledgeville. He did not last very long. He died in early February 1941 at the age of forty-five.

Flannery O'Connor wrote very little about her father. But when she did, she wrote tenderly of him. "I really only knew him by a kind of instinct,"[21] she wrote when she was thirty-one and afflicted with the same disease that killed him. Whereas Regina expressed her love by a highly efficient ordering of her daughter's life, by ensuring that she had every opportunity and advantage, Edward seems to have expressed his love in simple delight. He encouraged her creativity and carried around her childhood cartoons and stories to show to his friends. Surrounded by ferociously efficient women, Flannery O'Connor saw in her father a kindred spirit, for better or for worse: "I am never likely to romanticize him," she said, "because I carry around most of his faults as well as his tastes."[22]

Flannery O'Connor thought of her father as a frustrated writer, a man who would have written more than American Legion speeches if he had not been burdened by the responsibilities of family life that she herself never had. She wrote,

> Needing people badly and not getting them may turn you in a creative direction, provided you have the other requirements. [Father] needed the people I guess and got them. Or rather wanted them and got them. I wanted them and didn't. . . . Whatever I do in the way of writing makes me extra happy in the thought that it is a fulfillment of what he wanted to do himself.[23]

The father who was absent in so many ways, then, was forever present in her work.

2 | "MOSTLY SHE TALKED FLANNERY": MILLEDGEVILLE, 1939–1945

Milledgeville, like Savannah, is a place where a sense of history is strong. Stately antebellum mansions remind the visitor of each town's importance during the Civil War: Milledgeville was Georgia's capital, and Savannah was the state's largest population center and most important port. General Sherman came to both towns on his March to the Sea.

For all their Old South echoes, however, Milledgeville and Savannah were and are very different places. In 1940, Savannah boasted almost 100,000 residents, whereas Milledgeville had fewer than seven thousand. Savannah, while distinctly Southern, also had the cosmopolitan flavor of any seaport. Nestled in rolling red clay hills of Middle Georgia, Milledgeville's Southern sensibilities were not tempered by the outside cultural influences of the port city.

Which is not to say that Milledgeville was an altogether typical small Southern town. Milledgeville is a college town;

the Georgia State College for Women (GSCW)—now Georgia College and State University—was only one block from the Cline house. Milledgeville was also home to a military school, a reform school, and an insane asylum. In Middle Georgia "going to Milledgeville" is still a euphemism for going crazy. There is more than one kind of cultural diversity.

Ironically, the move to the smaller town broadened Mary Flannery in ways that would be important to her writing career. While there was a Catholic population in Milledgeville and a Catholic church—Sacred Heart—there was no Catholic quarter as there was in Savannah. Unlike the neighbors on Lafayette Square, the O'Connors' neighbors in Milledgeville were almost all Protestant. Here began O'Connor's close observation of the varieties of Protestantism that inform her fiction of the "Christ-haunted" South.

There was no parish school attached to Sacred Heart Church, so Mary Flannery attended Peabody Model School, on the campus of GSCW. Peabody was set up as a place where student teachers at GSCW's Peabody Normal School (the school of education) could get teaching experience and observe the latest teaching methods. Peabody was a far cry from the nun-governed rigidity of St. Vincent's and Sacred Heart in Savannah. O'Connor had "certain grim memories of days and months of just 'hanging out' in school."[1] Strongly influenced by John Dewey and his disciple William Heard Kilpatrick, the teachers at Peabody valued the students' preferences in ways the nuns never had—and in ways that O'Connor herself did not approve of. The teachers, she told a friend,

> asked us what, as mature children, we thought we ought to study. At that school we were always "planning." They would

as soon have given us arsenic in the drinking fountains as let us study Greek. I know no history whatsoever. We studied that hindside foremost, beginning with the daily paper and tracing problems from it backward.[2]

O'Connor never had anything good to say about the school that gave her more freedom than she even wanted. "I'm blessed with Total Non-Retention," she wrote, "which means I have not been harmed by a sorry education—or that is my cheerful way of viewing it."[3]

The social awkwardness that characterized O'Connor in elementary school survived into high school. She showed little interest in boys and did little to ingratiate herself to the girls either. Jean Cash interviewed a high school acquaintance of O'Connor's who spoke of the rejection that O'Connor experienced—rejection that she brought on herself to some degree by her aloofness and her refusal to play well with others:

> I am not proud to say that I and my friends were unkind to Mary Flannery. She was always excluded from parties. Her Connecticut cousins visited during the summer and there were parties for them and she had to be included. She spent the evening in a corner by herself. She was physically unattractive and we (I) didn't explore her mind.[4]

O'Connor was not a recluse, however. She found a niche in the school newspaper, for which she wrote and drew cartoons—somewhat crude and angular linocuts of students daydreaming at their desks or sitting backward on a desk or bolting for the exit in cap and gown. Her cartoons exhibited very little in the way of rah-rah enthusiasm or even the most basic school spirit.

O'Connor did well at Peabody, especially in her English classes. In her leisure time she continued to write, barnyard fowl still figuring largely into her creative efforts. A seventeen-page illustrated poem called "Mistaken Identity" told the story of a rather dashing gander named Herman who, upon laying an egg, had to be renamed Henrietta. Herman/Henrietta's story was based on a true story from Mary Flannery's own collection of birds.

She may not have been popular, but Mary Flannery was at least interesting enough as a senior in high school to be the subject of a profile in the Peabody school newspaper. "Peabodite Reveals Strange Hobby," the headline read. The hobby in question was collecting publishers' rejection slips, though it is not clear if she had actually sent off her stories about geese and chickens to any publishers or if she was joking. In any case, according to the article, her ambition even in high school was to "keep right on writing, particularly satires."[5]

The article, not surprisingly, had much to say about O'Connor's birds—chickens with names like Hitler and Hailie Selassie, a crow named Winston, the gander Herman who unexpectedly laid eight eggs. The article also mentions her collection of 150 china and glass chickens, her musical accomplishments (clarinet, accordion, and "bull fiddle"), her work as cartoonist for the school newspaper, and her hobby of making lapel pins that she sold in a local store. The freewheeling academic environment of Peabody Model School left her ample time, it seems, to pursue her various interests and hobbies.

O'Connor graduated from Peabody in May 1942. When she "went off" to college, she didn't go any farther than she had gone for high school. She enrolled at GSCW and continued to live with her mother and aunts a block from the campus.

O'Connor later said that while she "despised" high school, she enjoyed her college experience. Nevertheless, she was still dismissive of the education she received there. "I didn't really start to read until I went to Graduate School," she claimed. "When I went to Iowa I had never heard of Faulkner, Kafka, Joyce, much less read them."[6]

O'Connor seems, however, to have matured socially, at least a little bit. She made more and closer friends than she had earlier in life. Most of her friends, according to one of her classmates, were involved in student government, the literary magazine, and the annual. One of the closest was Betty Boyd (later Betty Boyd Love). Having met in the earliest days of their freshman year, they worked together on the *Corinthian* literary magazine. Betty was a frequent visitor at the Cline house. She wrote of O'Connor,

> She knew who she was, and what she was, and was neither over-pleased nor disturbed by either. There are critics who would have you believe that she was something of a freak herself. Not so! She was physically a bit awkward. She may have considered some social conventions absurd. But she never exhibited any open rebellion. She was probably merely amused. She "talked Southern," to use her own words. Well, yes, in a way—but mostly she talked Flannery. She drawled, she had a wry twist of humor, and she was delightful company.[7]

At GSCW O'Connor was a bit of a campus personality. Sarah Gordon wrote about her "loping gait and brusque salute" and her habit of "calling out 'Greetings!' instead of the customary 'Hey' or 'Hello' to her classmates."[8]

O'Connor's cartoons appeared regularly in the *Colonnade* campus newspaper, the *Corinthian* literary magazine, and

GSCW's yearbook, the *Spectrum*. She signed her college cartoons with the initials MFOC arranged in the shape of a stick-figure chicken. Her linocut technique in these cartoons showed considerable improvement over her high school work. Her figures, with their bulging eyes and sloping noses, appear to have been influenced by the work of *New Yorker* cartoonist James Thurber. As a college student, in fact, she submitted some of her cartoons to the *New Yorker*, though her submissions were rejected.[9]

O'Connor's college-era cartoons exhibit a sense of satire that will come into sharper focus in her fiction. They have about them an insider's perspective that her high school cartoons never exhibited. The jokes are often inside jokes that are lost on the outsider. As is often the case in college newspaper cartoons, the subjects tend to be topical—the Golden Slipper dance contest, a shortage of classroom space, the faculty softball game. By far the most frequent topic of O'Connor's cartoons was the invasion of Navy WAVES (Women's Auxiliary Volunteer Emergency Service) on GSCW's campus. The fifteen thousand WAVES who were housed and trained at GSCW from 1943 through the end of World War II were O'Connor's most immediate and tangible reminder that her country was at war. From the WAVES' arrival on campus until their (and O'Connor's) departure in 1945, more than a third of O'Connor's cartoons for the *Colonnade* were concerned with the WAVES, typically contrasting the WAVES' naval spit and polish with the students' more relaxed habits.

At GSCW, O'Connor was enrolled in a special wartime fast-track program by which she would attend class through the summers and complete her degree in three years. She was still seventeen years old and less than two weeks out of high school when she entered college. She was only nineteen when she finished in the spring of 1945, shortly after the end of the war in Europe.

O'Connor's grades were good; she was on the dean's list every quarter of her college career but one. She majored in social science rather than English, perhaps to avoid the meddling of English teachers who knew less about writing than she did; a few of her teachers tried and failed to convince her to write in a more "ladylike" manner.

Late in her career at GSCW, O'Connor took a philosophy class with a new professor named George Beiswanger. He quickly saw in O'Connor an unusual brilliance and independence of mind as she engaged the modern philosophers from a Catholic perspective. "Flannery sat in class, listened intently, took notes," Beiswanger said, "and without saying a word, it became clear that she didn't believe a word of what I was saying. . . . She knew Aquinas in detail, was amazingly well read in earlier philosophy, and developed into a first rate '*intellectual*' along with her other accomplishments. . . . It soon became clear to me that she was a 'born' writer and that she was going that way."[10]

Beiswanger had earned his PhD at the University of Iowa. He convinced his stubborn but brilliant student to apply for graduate school there, offering to write her a recommendation. She took his advice and applied to the journalism school with a view toward continuing her cartooning career.

She was accepted at Iowa. At the age of nineteen, O'Connor prepared to move away from Georgia for the first time in her life and set about the business of becoming a writer in earnest.

3 | "I BEGAN TO READ EVERYTHING AT ONCE": IOWA, 1945–1948

When Mary Flannery O'Connor went to Iowa City, she decided to take a new name to go along with the start of her new life outside Georgia. She dropped "Mary." Henceforth she would be known as Flannery O'Connor to all but family and old acquaintances.

The name change did not, however, signify a desire to reinvent herself entirely. She still attended Mass nearly every day, walking the quarter mile from her dormitory in Currier Hall to St. Mary's Church. "I went there three years and never knew a soul in that congregation or any of the priests," she wrote, "but it was not necessary. As soon as I went in the door I was home."[1] Nearly every day she lived away from Georgia, she wrote to her mother (often a mere postcard) and she read the Milledgeville newspapers that her mother regularly sent.

O'Connor had only been on the University of Iowa campus a few days when she made her way to the office of Paul Engle, director of the Iowa Writers' Workshop. Having been established in 1936, the Iowa Writers' Workshop was the first institution in the United States to offer a Master of Fine Arts in English—a degree for which the culminating work is a novel or collection of stories or poems rather than a thesis or dissertation. Even today, the Workshop remains one of the most important training grounds for American writers. Since 1936, twenty-eight Pulitzer Prizes have gone to its graduates or faculty members.

Paul Engle often told the story of his first meeting with Flannery O'Connor, though he didn't always tell it the same way. In a letter to Robert Giroux, O'Connor's editor and publisher, Engle recalled that a very young woman (she was still a teenager at the time) came to his office and started talking to him in a Georgia accent so thick that he couldn't understand what she was saying. It was so bad, in fact, that he asked her to write down whatever it was that she was trying to say. "My name is Flannery O'Connor," she wrote. "I am not a journalist. Can I come to the Writers' Workshop?"

Engle read some of O'Connor's work, and she was soon in the program. "The stories were quietly filled with insight, shrewd about human weakness, hard and compassionate," he wrote.[2]

O'Connor had always been serious about her studies, but at Iowa she found for the first time a genuine match between her talent and vocation and the training that was on offer. At GSCW she had majored in social science; her English professors recognized her brilliance, but there was little they could do for her. She was beyond them before she ever got there. In Iowa she was finally among people who were like-minded and—more to the point—who were farther down the road than she was. At Iowa, there were people who could teach her something about writing.

O'Connor applied herself to the work with tremendous focus. Paul Engle wrote:

The will to be a writer was adamant; nothing could resist it, not even her own sensibility about her own work. Cut, alter, try it again . . . sitting at the back of the room, silent, Flannery was more of a presence than the exuberant talkers who serenade every writing-class with their loudness. [3]

She was implacably serious about writing better, and neither ego nor false modesty got in her way.

When experienced fiction writers like Robert Penn Warren and Andrew Lytle—both guest lecturers in Iowa—offered good advice, she took it, more interested in writing better than in defending her position. O'Connor was supremely confident in her writerly gifts, but she didn't consider herself infallible, and she was always open to any advice that would help her be truer to her artistic vision. On the other hand, according to her friend Robie Macauley, she didn't always take the advice of Engle, who thought of her as his protégé. She considered his suggestions about *Wise Blood* to be far from the mark. [4]

Encouraged by Paul Horgan, an instructor at the Workshop, O'Connor began to establish the disciplined writing habits that were a cornerstone of her work and life for the rest of her days. As she wrote to a friend years later, "I'm a full-time believer in writing habits, pedestrian as it all may sound. You may be able to do without them if you have genius but most of us only have talent and this is simply something that has to be assisted all the time by physical and mental habits or it dries up and blows away." [5]

If she had been under-read in her prior life, O'Connor began to make up for it in Iowa. "Then I began to read everything at once," she wrote, "so much so that I didn't have time to be influenced by any one writer." The native genius that had been hitherto shaped by Uncle Remus and *The Humorous Tales of E. A. Poe* (as well as Aquinas and the ancients) was now being redirected by the Catholic novelists François Mauriac, Georges Bernanos, Léon Bloy, Graham Greene, and Evelyn Waugh; by the Southern writers William Faulkner, Allen Tate, Caroline Gordon Tate, Katherine Anne Porter, Eudora Welty, and Peter Taylor; by the Russians Dostoyevsky, Turgenev, Chekhov, and Gogol; even by "nuts" like Djuna Barnes, Dorothy Richardson, and Virginia Woolf. She read Hawthorne (whose use of the term "romance" in place of "novel" she admired), Flaubert, Conrad, Balzac, and Kafka. Later, critics would compare her work to Kafka's, though she insisted that she had never finished reading anything that Kafka wrote.[6]

Perhaps surprisingly, O'Connor was strongly influenced by a textbook: *Understanding Fiction* by the aforementioned Robert Penn Warren and Cleanth Brooks. Later in life she spoke dismissively of an academic approach to writing and literature; earlier, perhaps, *Understanding Fiction* was the first book she had seen that distilled her own instincts for storytelling into a set of guidelines.

It was quickly apparent that even in the rarefied air of the Iowa Writers' Workshop, Flannery O'Connor was something special, possessed of a talent that was well beyond that of her very talented peers. As writers came through to teach, they paid her particular attention. Andrew Lytle, who directed the Workshop during O'Connor's last semester there, described her as the "only student there with exceptional talent." John Crowe Ransom read one of her stories to the class when he visited, though he balked at her use of the word "nigger." He said "negro" instead. "It did spoil the story," O'Connor told Robie Macauley. "The people I was writing about would never use any other word."[7]

But if the teachers gave her particular attention, her classmates—mostly men and mostly war veterans—tended to snub the very young and inexperienced woman in their midst. The men in the class mostly wrote war stories, and they enjoyed one another's work, at the expense of the work of the three women in the class. None of those men, however, went on to any particular distinction as writers. Kay Buford, one of the two other women in the class, recalled at least one episode in which one of O'Connor's stories received less attention than it deserved. She also remembered, however, that O'Connor showed little interest in anybody else's work, which might do as much to explain her male colleagues' reaction to her as any sexism on their part.[8]

It wasn't long before O'Connor's writing began to get recognition beyond the Workshop. In February 1946—her second semester at Iowa—she sent a story called "The Geranium" to the journal *Accent*. It was accepted. She was not yet twenty-one years old.

"The Geranium" is a country-come-to-town story, a story of almost pathological homesickness, in which a displaced white Southerner is undone by the very different social mores of New York City. The story deals with themes that would shape O'Connor's fiction for the rest of her life. Indeed, the last story she completed before she died was a reworking of this, her first published story.

That fall, O'Connor began working on a novel. The short story she called "The Train," after considerable revision, would eventually become the first chapter of *Wise Blood*. Home from the army, Hazel Wickers (his last name would become Motes) gets sideways with a black train porter he believes to be from his hometown of Eastrod, Tennessee. The porter is considerably more dignified than the rube who tries to insult and condescend to him. Hazel is coming home to a whole new world. He has no home, in fact. The few families who remained in Eastrod when he went away have left by the time he comes back. His mother is dead. And he is headed to the big city of Taulkinham, where his older sister lives, a place as strange to him as Persia. Hazel is a man on the move with no place to go.

"The Geranium" and "The Train" were two of six stories that comprised O'Connor's master's thesis, which she submitted in May 1947. The other stories were "The Barber," "Wildcat," "The Crop," and "The Turkey." They are impressive work for a writer as young as Flannery O'Connor, who turned twenty-two the spring she finished her MFA. Themes and situations that would absorb her the rest of her life are here in the collection: race, class, the conflict of an intellectualized view of the world and the self on the one hand and folk wisdom on the other, with folk wisdom carrying the day every time.

But still, the stories are in essence juvenilia; O'Connor was still looking for her voice when she wrote these stories. "The Crop," while it has the biting humor of O'Connor's later writing, is scarcely recognizable as an O'Connor story. But even the stories that *are* recognizably O'Connor are O'Connor in an attenuated form. As in her later stories, her characters are subject to painful realizations in the end, but the stakes seem not so high; the sudden unveiling of truth at the end may hit a character like a two-by-four, but not like a thunderstroke, as it does in her mature stories. In these early stories, O'Connor is only just beginning to harness the verbal and symbolic power, the apocalyptic vision that make her work so unique. As Paul Elie put it, "Something vital is missing in these stories. They are all manners and no mystery."[9]

O'Connor's work was good enough, however, for publication. The *Sewanee Review* bought "The Train," and *Mademoiselle* bought "The Turkey." Both were published in 1948. Even more significantly, "The Train," along with three other chapters of

Wise Blood, won O'Connor the prestigious Rinehart-Iowa Award. Rinehart Publishing awarded her $750—an impressive amount considering that O'Connor's scholarship stipend at the time was $20 per month (which was itself a raise from the $60 per semester she received during her first year at Iowa). In exchange, Rinehart had the right of first refusal on the novel when O'Connor finished it.

Upon finishing her MFA in the spring of 1947, O'Connor was awarded a fellowship that allowed her to return to Iowa for post-graduate study. She continued working on her novel that year. She also began to make important literary friendships that would last the rest of her life. Robie Macauley was an expert on Russian literature and a graduate of Kenyon College in Ohio, where he had been a disciple of John Crowe Ransom. Besides being an academic, Macauley had also spent some time in the publishing world, having been an editor at Henry Holt.

Macauley and O'Connor hit it off immediately. In later years, Macauley spoke of "dating" O'Connor in Iowa, though he clarified that there was no real romantic attachment. Macauley, it appears, played an important role in O'Connor's social development. She had always been painfully awkward in social situations, always seeming to say the wrong thing. Macauley, according to mutual friend Walter Sullivan, took some of the edge off O'Connor and helped her relax in social situations. O'Connor eventually developed a gift for friendship, especially with bookish people, who had been in short supply when she was growing up. Taking her to parties, introducing her to his literary friends, Macauley helped O'Connor develop that latent gift.[10]

At the beginning of 1948, Andrew Lytle, the editor of the *Sewanee Review*, came to Iowa City to direct the Workshop in the absence of Paul Engle, who was on sabbatical. He oversaw

O'Connor's work on her novel. As a guest lecturer a year or two earlier, he had recognized the young writer's genius, but he was still a little squeamish about her work. "Fiction about rednecks turned him off, I believe," said Macauley.[11] By the time *Wise Blood* was published in 1952, it was very different from the book Lytle helped O'Connor with; he didn't especially like the end result and declined when the editor of *Shenandoah* asked him to review it. "I don't now know what I think about it," he wrote. He was putt off by the book's persistent interest in religion: "There is a move towards the Old Church on the part of some of my friends, and I'm afraid extraneous zeal is confusing their artistry."[12]

But whatever Lytle thought of the finished product, in the spring of 1948 he gladly recommended O'Connor for a summer residency at the Yaddo artist's colony in Saratoga Springs, New York. O'Connor, he wrote, showed "as much promise as anyone I have seen of her generation."[13] O'Connor was accepted. She left for New York in early June 1948, planning to return to Iowa in the fall for a yearlong teaching fellowship.

As it turned out, she would never again be in a university setting except as a guest lecturer. Her contributions thenceforth would be as an author rather than an academic.

4 | "THE PECULIARITY ... OF THE EXPERIENCE I WRITE FROM": NEW YORK AND CONNECTICUT, 1948–1950

Outside the New York publishing houses themselves, if there was one place closer to the center of American letters than the Iowa Writers' Workshop, that place was Yaddo artists' colony. Built on four hundred acres in Saratoga Springs, New York, Yaddo was set aside as a place where working artists, from writers to composers to visual artists, could do their work "without interruption in a supportive environment."

Yaddo's founders were Spencer and Katrina Trask. Spencer was a Gilded Age financier—a financial backer of Thomas Edison and president of the company that became Consolidated Edison, the world's first power company. Katrina was a poet. When the death of their four children left them without close heirs, the Trasks decided to leave their country estate to future generations of writers and artists. A *Time* magazine article from 1938 described the moment in 1899 when Katrina Trask had a vision of Yaddo's future while walking with her husband through the estate's wildwood:

> Here will be a perpetual series of house parties—of literary men, literary women, and other artists. . . . At Yaddo they will find the Sacred Fire, and light their torches at its flame. Look, Spencer! They are walking in the woods, wandering in the garden, sitting under the pine trees . . . creating, creating, creating![1]

Katrina Trask would likely have been pleased with the outworking of her vision. As of 2011, Yaddo writers have won sixty-six Pulitzer Prizes, sixty-one National Book Awards, twenty-four National Book Critics Circle Awards, and a Nobel Prize.

Elizabeth Ames was the director of Yaddo in O'Connor's era. She had near-dictatorial control over who came to Yaddo and how long they were allowed to stay; but she was attentive to the artists' needs when they were there, and she ran the place with great efficiency.

The setting made a most favorable impression on Flannery O'Connor. Encouraging her friend Cecil Dawkins to apply for a fellowship some ten years later, she spoke of its blandishments: "The food is very good. The quarters are elegant. The servants are very nice. The scenery is magnificent."[2] Everything about the Yaddo experience was designed to give the artist the liberty to create. Every need and comfort was attended to. In addition to her sleeping quarters, O'Connor was assigned a studio—though, as she told Cecil Dawkins, she would have preferred just to write in her room. After breakfast each morning, the artists went to their studios to work, a packed lunch pail in hand. A monastic silence was enforced during working hours.

Besides the liberty to create, the residents of Yaddo took other liberties as well. The artists were a hard-drinking crowd, and they threw frequent parties. O'Connor said she attended one or two of these parties "but always left before they began to break things." In her Yaddo primer for Cecil Dawkins, she spoke disapprovingly of Yaddo's sexual mores: "In such a place you have to expect them all to sleep around. This is not sin but Experience, and if you do not sleep with the opposite sex, it is assumed that you sleep with your own. . . . At the breakfast table they talked about Seconal and barbiturates and now maybe it's marijuana."[3] O'Connor attended Mass with the domestic help, whom she considered the moral superiors of the artists they served. She seemed to feel she had more in common with the help than with her fellow artists. "After a few weeks at Yaddo," O'Connor observed, "you long to talk to an insurance salesman, dog-catcher, bricklayer—anybody who isn't talking about Form or sleeping pills."[4]

There were plenty of artists at Yaddo who were not producing. O'Connor warned her friend against getting swept into the extracurriculars: "You survive in this atmosphere by minding your own business and by having plenty of your own business to mind; and by not being afraid to be different from the rest of them."[5] O'Connor certainly minded her business at Yaddo. She made the most of her six-week summer appointment, extensively rewriting two chapters of *Wise Blood*—the chapters published independently as "The Peeler" and "The Heart of the Park." The novel really began to take shape at Yaddo. Here O'Connor's cast of country-come-to town-zealots and hucksters and sideshow freaks began to come together.

"The Peeler" is the chapter in which we first meet Enoch

Emery, as well as Asa and Sabbath Lily Hawks. The setting is urban, though many of the characters are rural. In this early piece of *Wise Blood*, Enoch is much more vivid than Hazel Motes, the novel's main character. Motes is on the run from Jesus in these early chapters, but he is not the antiprophet that he becomes in the final version. In the next two chapters that were published as stories—"A Stroke of Good Fortune" and "Enoch and the Gorilla," Hazel Motes is still mostly absent. He would not be fully imagined until after O'Connor left Yaddo.

O'Connor had scarcely settled into her room at Yaddo before, on the recommendation of a fellow Yaddo writer, she wrote a letter to the agent Elizabeth McKee. She took the direct approach: "Dear Miss McKee," she wrote, "I am looking for an agent."

McKee agreed to take O'Connor on as a client. They maintained their client-agent relationship—and their friendship—through the rest of O'Connor's life. McKee's partner was an older woman named Mavis McIntosh, who had been John Steinbeck's first agent. Ever the master of the telling detail, O'Connor once described her agents to Maryat Lee thus: "Miss McIntosh is an old lady who sits at her desk with her hat on and Miss McKee is a youngish lady who speaks out of the side of her mouth like a refined dead-end kid."[6]

When O'Connor's six-week stint at Yaddo was finished at the end of July, Elizabeth Ames invited her to come back in September and stay through the end of the year. She had already been offered a teaching fellowship at Iowa, but she declined it in favor of the opportunity to return to Yaddo—a decision that did not please her very practical-minded mother.[7]

After spending six weeks in Georgia, O'Connor returned to a much smaller group of Yaddo artists in mid-September. There were only fifteen guests, among them Elizabeth Hardwick, a novelist and writer for the *Partisan Review*; Malcolm Cowley, a *New Republic* editor, Yaddo board member, and veteran of the Paris American-expatriate scene of the 1920s; and Robert "Cal" Lowell, a poet and rising literary star.

The good-looking Lowell was by far the most magnetic of the group at Yaddo that fall. A Catholic convert from a Boston Brahmin family, he had won a Pulitzer Prize for poetry the previous year. As a student he eschewed the Ivy League—the obvious path for a Bostonian of his social station—choosing instead to attend Kenyon College, where Allen Tate and John Crowe Ransom held court. Lowell was given to the grand gesture. When he first arrived at Kenyon, he jokingly asked Tate if he could live with him. Tate jokingly replied that he was welcome to pitch a tent in his yard, so Lowell bought a pup tent, set it up in the Tates's yard, and lived there for two months.

Lowell took a liking to Flannery O'Connor, immediately recognizing her talent. Brad Gooch's summary is helpful: "Lowell's feelings for Flannery were not romantic, but they were full of excitement for her Roman Catholicism and her rare brand of Southern literary talent."[8] O'Connor, for her part, felt strongly about the handsome poet, though it is not obvious whether her feelings were romantic. "He is one of the people I love," she once told Betty Hester.[9]

O'Connor worked on her novel through the fall, learning in mid-October that she was welcome to stay until March. By wintertime, the fifteen residents had dwindled down to five: O'Connor and four men, including Cal Lowell.

Though Lowell had converted to Catholicism during his first marriage, to Jean Stafford, he was a lapsed Catholic by the time he arrived at Yaddo. But during that winter, due in part no doubt to the influence of Flannery O'Connor, he began a slow process of returning to the Catholic faith. "I watched him that winter come back into the Church," she said. "I had nothing to do with it but of course it was a great joy to me."[10]

Rather than going home for Christmas, O'Connor spent the break at Yaddo. The new year, 1949, brought Elizabeth Hardwick back to the artists' colony. Hardwick and Lowell and O'Connor became something of a trio. O'Connor watched Lowell and Hardwick fall in love and eventually marry some months after they left Yaddo.

O'Connor continued to use her time well at the artists' colony. By January she had drafted nine of fourteen chapters of *Wise Blood*. Rinehart's John Selby had indicated that he would not be willing to discuss a contract until he had seen a full draft of the book. O'Connor, however, asked Elizabeth McKee to forward the nine chapters to Selby and see if he would be willing to negotiate an advance based on the work she had already done.

Part of O'Connor's eagerness derived from the fact that another publisher had expressed interest in *Wise Blood*. Alfred Kazin, a Yaddo friend, was a consultant to Harcourt, Brace. He had spoken of her work to Harcourt editor Robert Giroux, and Giroux, on the strength of the two chapters that had been published, was interested. O'Connor was eager to get an answer from Selby and see how things would play out.

Selby was not especially taken with the nine chapters he saw. He indicated a number of revisions that he would require before he would be willing to publish the book. O'Connor in the past had demonstrated a willingness to hear intelligent criticism and to take it seriously. But Selby's suggestions—and his tone—got all over her. He completely missed the point of her book, she believed, and he was condescending into the bargain. She wrote to McKee, "The letter is addressed to a slightly dim-witted Camp

Fire Girl, and I cannot look with composure on getting a lifetime of others like them."[11]

McKee and O'Connor agreed that it would be best for O'Connor to have a conversation with Selby in person rather than trying to work things out via letter. But according to O'Connor's experience, Selby tended to say "as little as possible as vaguely as possible." So she wrote him a letter with the intention of giving him something concrete to respond to:

> I feel that whatever virtues the novel may have are very much connected with the limitations you mention. I am not writing a conventional novel, and I think that the quality of the novel I write will derive precisely from the peculiarity or aloneness, if you will, of the experience I write from. . . . In short, I am amenable to criticism but only within the sphere of what I am trying to do; I will not be persuaded to do otherwise. The finished book, though I hope less angular, will be just as odd if not odder than the nine chapters you have now. The question is: is Rinehart interested in publishing this kind of novel?[12]

When O'Connor and Selby met the next week, they remained at an impasse. O'Connor told Selby that she would be willing to *listen* to criticism from Rinehart's editors, but she refused to be bound by any of it. And what was even more of an impasse, O'Connor didn't feel she could write any more without getting more money than the $750 the publisher had already paid through the Rinehart-Iowa prize. But Selby was unwilling to give her any more money without seeing the finished book.

Summarizing the matter for Paul Engle, she wrote, "I will not be hurried or directed by Rinehart. I think they are interested in the conventional and I have had no indication that they are very bright. I feel the heart of the matter is they don't care to lose $750 (or as they put it, Seven Hundred and Fifty Dollars)."[13]

She told Engle, "Selby and I came to the conclusion that I was 'prematurely arrogant.' I supplied the phrase." The encouragement she had received from Giroux at Harcourt made her itchy to get free from Rinehart's option.

Right in the middle of the Selby blowup, O'Connor found herself involved in another fiasco at Yaddo. Cal Lowell, politically conservative by the standards of East Coast writer types, had grown troubled by the presence at Yaddo of a novelist and journalist named Agnes Smedley. A personal friend of Elizabeth Ames, Smedley had stayed on at Yaddo at Ames's pleasure for five very unproductive years. Besides being a friend of Ames, she was also a Communist sympathizer and had been accused by the army of being a Soviet spy. The army quickly retracted the accusation, though subsequent revelations suggest that she was indeed a spy.[14]

Lowell smelled impropriety; he met with Yaddo's board to demand that Ames be fired. The board did not dismiss Lowell's claims, but scheduled a hearing, in which Lowell served as the prosecuting attorney, examining and cross-examining witnesses, including Flannery O'Connor. In the end, the board sided with Ames; the four remaining residents—Lowell, Hardwick, O'Connor, and Edward Maisel—abruptly left the artists' colony.

O'Connor, like Elizabeth Hardwick and Cal Lowell, left for New York City. O'Connor stayed for a short while at Hardwick's apartment before securing a room of her own at a YMCA residence on 38th Street at Lexington Avenue, for two dollars a day.

O'Connor had scarcely been in New York a week when Cal Lowell started acting even stranger than usual. On Ash Wednesday, according to Lowell's own description, the conversion that had begun in previous months was complete and he "received the shock of the eternal word." He "returned to the Church . . . in an incredible outpouring of grace."[15] It soon became apparent, however, that mental imbalance was at work in Lowell. Somehow in his fevered religious imaginings he came to view Flannery O'Connor as a saint. In a March 4 phone call to Robert Fitzgerald he announced, "Today is the day of Flannery O'Connor, whose patron saint is Therese of Lisieux." He believed himself to be a prophet; he told Robert Fitzgerald to find a pencil and paper to write down the visions he described over the phone.

Alfred Kazin put Lowell's mania in context of other great poets of other eras: "He was at the top of a psychic crest down which he would slide the next season; but at this peak he talked in tongues; he was of the great company, with Milton and Hardy and Eliot."[16] Lowell's rantings were soon the talk of New York literary circles. For O'Connor, it was her nearest look at the kind of religious mania that would soon begin to appear in her fiction.

Years later, a friend found out about this episode with the insane Lowell and asked O'Connor about it. "I feel almost too much about him to be able to get to the heart of it," O'Connor wrote. "He is a kind of grief to me."[17] Not long after his "re-conversion," Lowell was confined to an insane asylum. O'Connor described the events:

> At the time it was happening, poor Cal was about three steps from the asylum. He had the delusion that he had been called on some kind of mission of purification and he was canonizing everybody that had anything to do with his situation then. . . . In a couple of weeks he was safely locked up. It would be funny if it had not been so terrible. . . . Things went faster and faster and faster for him until I guess the shock table took care of it.

It was a grief for me as if he had died. When he came out of it, he was no longer a Catholic.[18]

Before he lost his sanity, Lowell introduced O'Connor to two people who would be among the most important in her life. Robert and Sally Fitzgerald were bookish and devoutly Catholic. Robert was a translator, working at the time on *Oedipus Rex*. He described his first meeting with Flannery O'Connor in a preface to the short story collection *Everything That Rises Must Converge*: "We saw a shy Georgia girl, her face heart-shaped and pale and glum, with fine eyes that could stop frowning and open brilliantly upon everything. . . . Before she left that day we had a glimpse of her penetration and her scornful humor."[19]

The Fitzgeralds had been living with their two children in Manhattan, but they were ready to make a change. In the summer of 1949 they bought a house near Ridgefield, Connecticut. The house had a garage apartment. They needed a boarder to help pay the mortgage; they understood that Manhattan wasn't the place for Flannery O'Connor either. So they invited her to come live with them as a sort of paying houseguest.

Though the apartment above the Fitzgeralds' garage did not qualify as luxury accommodations, O'Connor found Connecticut much more to her liking than Manhattan. "Me and Enoch [from *Wise Blood*] are living in the woods in Connecticut with the Robert Fitzgeralds," she wrote to Robie Macauley. "Enoch didn't care so much for New York. He said there wasn't no privetcy there."[20]

O'Connor quickly settled into a routine. She rode to morning Mass with one of the Fitzgeralds (the other stayed home by turns to tend to the children). Back at the house, O'Connor worked through the morning. At noon she walked half a mile to fetch the mail and send the letter that she wrote every day to her mother.

In the afternoons, O'Connor babysat the Fitzgerald children. She ate her meals with the family. "They said the Benedictine grace before meals in Latin every day while the dinner got cold," O'Connor remarked. "I am more for expressing my appreciation by eating heartily while it's still warm."[21]

After the evening meal, when the children were put to bed, Sally and Robert and Flannery sat up talking over drinks. O'Connor regaled them with stories of life in Middle Georgia. She read pages from *Wise Blood* that she had written in the garage apartment. Robert told about his translation work. It was stimulating conversation, both entertaining and intellectual. The bookish talk energized O'Connor for her work. Those were productive days in Connecticut, writing and rewriting, resting and recovering. The Fitzgeralds created a near ideal environment for a writer like O'Connor, who needed to be left alone for hours at a time, but who also took sustenance from being part of a family. When a third Fitzgerald child was baptized, she was the godmother.

O'Connor was making excellent progress on her novel, but its publication status was still uncertain. At Rinehart, Selby had made no move to acquire the book, but neither had he released it. Meanwhile, Robert Giroux at Harcourt, Brace sent a provisional contract. O'Connor believed there was no legal barrier to her signing the Harcourt contract, but as a token of goodwill her agent sent a letter to Selby giving him one last chance to respond before O'Connor signed the Harcourt contract.

The release document that Selby finally sent described O'Connor as "stiff-necked, uncooperative and unethical."[22] O'Connor understandably viewed the language as insulting—a clear indication that she could never work with Selby. Nevertheless, in order to avoid even the appearance of unethical dealings, she offered to give Selby one last look at the manuscript in March, when she expected it to be close to completion. Harcourt and Giroux remained up in the air.

O'Connor went home to Milledgeville for Christmas 1949. While there, she had surgery to repair a "floating kidney"—a condition whereby a kidney moves around in the abdominal cavity, often causing significant discomfort. "I have to go to the hospital Friday and have a kidney hung on a rib,"[23] she joked in a letter to Elizabeth and Robert Lowell. The surgery was a success, and January found her back in Connecticut, resuming the work on her novel.

If 1949 had been the year of Enoch Emery, 1950 turned out to be the year of Hazel Motes. *Wise Blood*'s central character took shape in the Connecticut woods. Robert Fitzgerald wrote of an unexpected benefit of living with a translator of Greek tragedy: "In the summer of 1950, when she had reached an impasse with Haze and didn't know how to finish him off, she read for the first time the Oedipus plays. She went on then to end her story with the self-blinding of Motes, and she had to rework the body of the novel to prepare for it."[24]

In the winter of 1950, four years since she began writing, the first draft of *Wise Blood* was almost complete. Things were sorted out with the publishers; Rinehart decided not to exercise their option, while Giroux and Harcourt were glad to have the book.

While typing up the manuscript, just days before leaving again to spend Christmas in Milledgeville, O'Connor noticed that the act of typing produced in her arms a heaviness that she had never felt before. When it got worse, the Fitzgeralds took her to their doctor. The doctor said he thought the twenty-five-year-old writer had arthritis—perhaps rheumatoid arthritis—and encouraged her to get checked out at a hospital when she went back to Georgia for the holidays. No one had any idea how completely her life was about to change.

5 | "SICKNESS IS A PLACE": 1951–1952

In December 1950, Flannery O'Connor boarded a train that would take her from Connecticut to Georgia for a holiday visit with her family. She wore a beret at a jaunty angle—standard-issue headwear for the expatriate intellectual. Indeed, she seemed to be settling nicely into the role of Southern expatriate in Connecticut. She was never quite comfortable with the bohemian shenanigans of Yaddo, nor was Manhattan to her taste. But at Ridgefield she found a life that was both vigorously literary and cozily domestic. She was as engaged in the family life of the Fitzgeralds as she chose to be, but she also had time and space to do her work. And in the evenings she enjoyed the company and intellectual stimulation of like-minded friends. Equal parts literary genius and homebody—but also convinced that, for her art's sake, she needed to live somewhere besides home—O'Connor could hardly hope for a better situation.

Things were looking very good for the brilliant twenty-five-year-old whom Sally Fitzgerald put on the train in Connecticut.

O'Connor looked forward to a couple of weeks with home folks, then a return to her garret above the Fitzgeralds' garage for the homestretch of the novel with which she had been struggling since 1947. Fitzgerald remarked that O'Connor smiled "perhaps a little wanly" and she noticed "a kind of stiffness in her gait" but she looked "much as usual" when she saw her off.[1]

On the daylong train ride to Georgia, however, an aggressive fever settled into Flannery O'Connor's bones. When her uncle Louis Cline picked her up at the train station, she looked, he said, "like a shriveled old woman."

"I have never been anywhere but sick," O'Connor later wrote. "In a sense sickness is a place, more instructive than a long trip to Europe, and it's always a place where there's no company, where nobody can follow."[2] That train ride wasn't just a journey from Connecticut to Georgia. It was a journey into the land of sickness. There Flannery O'Connor would dwell for the rest of the thirteen and a half years that remained to her.

Uncle Louis took Flannery straight to Baldwin General Hospital in Milledgeville, where she was admitted. The initial diagnosis of her ailment was rheumatoid arthritis—a serious enough condition, possibly life-limiting, but not life-threatening. Her doctors put her on high doses of cortisone to counteract the inflammation in her joints.

O'Connor would spend the Christmas holidays and well beyond in the hospital. As was her custom, she treated the whole business as fodder for jokes and amusing anecdotes in her letters. She wrote to her old friend Betty Boyd,

> I am languishing on my bed of semi affliction, this time with AWTHRITUS [or], to give it all it has, *the* acute rheumatoid arthritis, what leaves you always willing to sit down, lie down,

lie flatter, etc. But I am taking cortisone so I will have to get up again. These days you caint even have you a good psychosomatic ailment to get yourself a rest.[3]

The humor, the understatement—this was no psychosomatic ailment that was keeping her in the hospital through Christmas—would be typical of Flannery O'Connor's talk about her sickness for the rest of her life. She was profligate with her humor; no doubt she used humor as a way of avoiding the hard realities of her situation once she came to understand how grave her situation was. But her very astute dramatic sense—that was something she stewarded and saved for her art. Even after she came to realize the seriousness of her condition, she never wasted her dramatic powers on self-dramatization. In that regard she was the opposite of a hypochondriac.

Low-grade fever often accompanies the inflammation of rheumatoid arthritis. But when the raging fevers continued weeks into the cortisone treatment, O'Connor's doctor suspected that she had something besides rheumatoid arthritis. He enlisted the help of internist and kidney expert Dr. Arthur J. Merrill of Atlanta's Emory University. Over the phone,[4] Dr. Merrill made a provisional diagnosis of systemic lupus erythematosus.

Shortly thereafter, in February, O'Connor was moved to Emory Hospital. Tests confirmed Dr. Merrill's telephone diagnosis: she had lupus, and a bad case of it. An autoimmune disorder, lupus is literally a kind of self-destruction. An overactive immune system attacks the tissues of its own body—skin, heart, lungs, kidneys, joints, nervous system. Since it can attack almost any bodily system in almost any combination, no two cases of lupus look alike, and the disorder often looks like some other disease, especially in the early stages. Even now, lupus is often misdiagnosed at first; rheumatoid arthritis, also an autoimmune disorder, is a frequent misdiagnosis. But whereas rheumatoid arthritis attacks primarily the tissues between the joints, lupus is more systemic, breaking down not only the joints, but every other system in the human body.

Dr. Merrill explained the gravity of the situation not to Flannery, but to her mother. At twenty-five, Flannery O'Connor was dying of the same disease that had killed her father ten years earlier.

Regina O'Connor believed that her daughter was in no condition to bear such heavy news. So she didn't tell her. She allowed Flannery to continue in her belief that she had rheumatoid arthritis. Regina did, however, call Sally Fitzgerald to report that Flannery had lupus. It would be another seventeen months before anyone told Flannery O'Connor the truth about the disease that was wracking her body.

The denial at work in those seventeen months would be hard to imagine if it weren't the sort of thing that happens all the time. Flannery O'Connor spent eight months in and out of Emory Hospital—mostly in. According to a letter she wrote years later (and in which, admittedly, she may have exaggerated), she received ten blood transfusions during February 1951. Doctors and nurses were coming and going, discussing dosages, writing on charts and whispering to her mother in the hallways. Flannery O'Connor was a woman of keen observation and highly active intelligence. She had watched her father die of lupus. Surely she knew there was something more serious at work in her body. And yet, as late as May 1952, she was still describing her ailment as arthritis.[5]

High-dose injections of the corticosteroid ACTH were the centerpiece of the treatment regimen for both rheumatoid arthritis and lupus. The injections gave limited relief to her physical symptoms, but they also swelled her features into a "moon-face" that made her self-conscious. Nor were the side effects of the injections strictly physical. As O'Connor told Robert Fitzgerald, "The large doses of ACTH send you off in a rocket and are scarcely less disagreeable than the disease."[6] Even in the hospital, however, O'Connor's artistic focus never wavered. She kept working on *Wise Blood* from her hospital bed. Disagreeable as the ACTH rocket-blast may have been, O'Connor credited it with helping her finish the book that had deviled her for so many years. "I was five years writing that book," she wrote to Betty Hester in 1955,

> and up to the last I was sure it was a failure and didn't work. When it was finished I came down with my energy-depriving ailment and began to take cortisone in large doses and cortisone makes you think night and day until I suppose the mind dies of exhaustion if you are not rescued.[7]

A long stretch on a sickbed is always an exercise in imagination. Who doesn't imagine how a serious illness will shape the rest of one's life or bring about one's death? O'Connor's imagination, already preternaturally active, was literally on steroids in the first months of 1951; in the midst of all that manic sickbed thinking, her imaginings of her own future melded with her imaginings of Hazel Motes, the protagonist of *Wise Blood*. She wrote,

> During this time I was more or less living my life and H. Mote's too and as my disease affected the joints, I conceived the notion that I would eventually become paralyzed and was going blind and that in the book I had spelled out my own course, or that in the illness I had spelled out the book.[8]

This flight of morbid fancy is virtually unique in the body of O'Connor's published correspondence. Elsewhere she is perfectly matter-of-fact in her descriptions of her life and especially her illness. This incursion of the literary into the world of her lived experience is significant not because it is typical but because it is so atypical of the way she talked about her life. She occasionally used autobiographical events as raw material for her fiction, but she seemed loath to use any of her artistic or imaginative energy to embroider her own story. At this moment of crisis, however, the personal and the creative interpenetrated one another, *Wise Blood* shaping the way O'Connor thought about her own future, her fears giving new intensity to Haze Motes's inner turmoil.

O'Connor finished a draft of *Wise Blood* probably in January 1951. Hazel Motes, the lost boy on the train in O'Connor's master's thesis, had become the fiery prophet of the "Church without Christ." His efforts to avoid Jesus, from self-righteousness to straightforward sins of the flesh, to the blasphemies of his preaching, finally even to cold, calculated murder, prove futile. Jesus, that "wild ragged figure" moving from tree to tree in the back of Hazel's mind, tracks him down in the end. The blasphemer is saved in spite of himself.

Not fully trusting her own instincts, O'Connor mailed a copy of *Wise Blood* to Robert Fitzgerald before giving it to Robert Giroux at Harcourt. Once Fitzgerald had assured her that her "Opus Nauseous" was as good as she hoped it was,[9] she sent it on to Giroux on March 10. "I hope you'll like it and decide to publish it," she wrote to him, with characteristic understatement.[10]

Shortly after the manuscript was off, the O'Connor women moved out of the Cline mansion in Milledgeville and into the house at Andalusia, the family's dairy farm four miles north of town. The town mansion had no groud-floor bedrooms, and Flannery's sickness made it hard to negotiate stairs. It was quiet at Andalusia; the dirt driveway running from the highway to the house was a quarter-mile long or longer, passing between a cow pasture on the right side and woods on the left. Large hardwoods shaded the yard immediately in front of the white two-story house with its full-length screened-in porch. Behind the house, chickens strutted and ducks waddled and fig trees spread their deep green leaves.

Andalusia was a working farm, and Regina worked hard at keeping things going. An unusually energetic woman, she was constantly on the move, dealing not only with the business of the farm itself, but also with the various crises and dramas of the families that were attached to the farm. White dairymen and their families came and went. As Flannery told a friend years later, "Off and on we find ourselves with some not-so-good country people but they are the type always on the move and we never have them for long."[11]

The black farmhands, however, who had fewer options in pre–civil rights Georgia, were more or less permanent. Regina's approach to her black employees especially was hands-on and generous, though also paternalistic in the manner of so many white employers of the pre–civil rights South. She was forever adjudicating arguments (sometimes violent arguments) or tending to the medical needs of her employees or their families, or helping them navigate one government bureaucracy or another, whether the legal system or the Department of Motor Vehicles.

Flannery, on the other hand, led a much more sedate life. The front parlor of the farmhouse was converted into a bedroom and writer's nook, and there she spent most of her time, waking and sleeping both. With its enforced quiet, the lifestyle of convalescence was amenable to the writing life. But to Flannery's mind, this time at Andalusia was a period of recovery, not her new routine. She was resigned to the possibility that it might take a long while to get back on her feet, but she had no intention of staying on the farm. She wrote to Robert Giroux, "I am up and around again now but won't be well enough to go back to Connecticut for some time."[12] There was some question as to when she would resume her life as the Southern expatriate, but she had every intention of going back north.

Six weeks after sending her manuscript to Harcourt, O'Connor still hadn't heard back from Giroux. The silence was surely deafening as she sat in that converted parlor day after day, a thousand miles away (both literally and figuratively) from New York or Ridgefield or Yaddo or Iowa. Andalusia didn't even have a telephone to connect her to the literary world that had come to feel like home.

She finally wrote to Elizabeth McKee to ask her to check in with the publisher, who had not even acknowledged receipt of the manuscript. "They ought to know by now if they want it or not," she wrote on April 24, "and I am anxious to get it off my mind."[13]

It would be June before O'Connor heard from McKee that Harcourt, Brace had accepted *Wise Blood* for publication. Her nerves still seem a little raw in her response to her agent: "I haven't heard from Bob Giroux but I suppose I will in whatever he considers the fullness of time."[14]

Even though the news from Harcourt took a load off her mind, new health concerns had presented themselves. Her symptoms had receded in the spring; she went down from four ACTH injections per day to one, which she administered herself. In April she reported to a friend that she was feeling better and looking better. But her symptoms flared again as the summer's heat bore down. She spent the summer in and out of the hospital.

Under those difficult circumstances, O'Connor still maintained her creative focus. She continued to live with *Wise Blood*, implementing revisions that Giroux suggested when he finally did get in touch with her. More important than her editor's edits, however, were the edits suggested by a new correspondent: Caroline Gordon.

Robert Fitzgerald had sent the manuscript of *Wise Blood* to Gordon—a Catholic novelist and literary critic—in hopes that her insights would be of benefit to O'Connor. A new Catholic (she and her husband, the poet Allen Tate, had both been recently baptized), Gordon had the zeal of a convert. Her deeply held literary convictions were now suffused with deeply held religious convictions; she saw it as her life's work to challenge and equip a new generation of Catholic writers. As Paul Elie put it, "No sooner had Gordon become a Catholic than she began calling for new Catholic fiction."[15]

From her first reading of *Wise Blood*, Gordon understood that O'Connor was exactly the kind of Catholic writer she was hoping would emerge. In a letter to Sally Fitzgerald she described O'Connor as "a rare phenomenon: a Catholic novelist with a real dramatic sense, one who relies more on her technique than her piety."[16]

Gordon made suggestions, which Fitzgerald passed on to O'Connor. O'Connor incorporated Gordon's edits along with Giroux's, writing in her changes on the manuscript and sending them along to a local woman who retyped from the beginning of the manuscript while she worked on later parts of the book.

In time, O'Connor would come to view the isolation of Andalusia and the limitations of her disease as beneficial, perhaps even necessary, to her creative process. In the letters she wrote during her first year or so back in Georgia, however, it is evident that she had not yet accepted her isolation as a good thing. "Me & Maw are still at the farm and are like to be, I perceive, through the winter," she wrote to the Fitzgeralds. "She is nuts about it out here, surrounded by the lowing herd and other details, and considers it beneficial to my health."[17] Regina may have been nuts about Andalusia, but Flannery's failure to mention her own opinion on the matter seems significant. And even though she reported that her health had improved, the opinion that the farm was beneficial to her health was expressed as her mother's, not hers.

In the same letter, O'Connor remarked that she had been reading old copies of the *Saturday Review* that she borrowed from an English-teacher friend. "The face of Malcolm Cowley shines out in every issue." It is possible, of course, that she was unreservedly happy for her old Yaddo friend in his success. But it is hard to imagine her not being at least a little wistful at the thought of Cowley—whom Robert Lowell described as "nice but a little slow"[18]—so close to the center of the literary world, and herself in a Georgia farmhouse, observing his success in borrowed magazines.

In Connecticut, her mornings of writing had been followed by evenings of conversation with book people who shared what they were reading and writing, who read her work with a critical eye and sharpened her craft thereby. Life at Andalusia had its charms, but literary stimulation was not one of them. Her mother did ask to read the *Wise Blood* manuscript once, but the experiment was less than a total success. "I found her half an hour later on page 9 and sound asleep," Flannery wrote the Fitzgeralds. When Flannery spent an afternoon devouring *The Catcher in the Rye*, Regina warned her that she would ruin her eyes reading so much in one day. That was what passed for literary conversation between the O'Connor women. "She likes books with [animal trainer and explorer] Frank Buck and a lot of wild animals," Flannery said of her mother.[19]

Her isolation seems to have shaken O'Connor's faith in her own aesthetic judgment; perhaps it was for the better. The same day in March when she sent her manuscript to the publisher, she wrote to Elizabeth McKee, "So far as I am concerned this is the last draft of the book, unless there is something really glaring in it that may be pointed out to me."[20] Her sense of finality may have had as much to do with her exhaustion after a five-year struggle with the book (not to mention her physical ailments) as with her actual artistic judgment. In any case, as the summer went on, she felt less and less sure that her work on *Wise Blood* was done or even almost done.

When she got the revision back from the typist in September 1951, she said that reading back through it "was like spending the day eating a horse blanket. It seems mighty sorry to me but better than it was."[21] In mid-October, she sent the revised manuscript back to Giroux with a caveat: "It looks better to me but I have no one here to read it who could tell me."[22]

But she knew who could tell her. She solicited further help from Caroline Gordon, who was delighted to give it. Gordon's second round of comments ran to nine single-spaced pages and looked as much like a manifesto as a set of editorial notes. Gordon, as was her wont, spoke of the writer's work in theological terms: "Theology takes cognizance of a soul only in its relation to God; its relation to its fellow-men in the end, helps to constitute its relations with God."[23] *Wise Blood*, Gordon understood, worked in the same way. Haze Motes is such a peculiar figure in large part because his relations with God are more fully realized than his relations with other characters. This is the source of much of the book's unique power. But it also presents unique problems for the fiction writer. The building blocks of fiction, after all, are visible, concrete, and outward, even if its aims are ultimately invisible, abstract, and inward. Many of Gordon's notes revolved around methods and techniques for bringing to life the surface of the story—the "scene," in Gordon's terminology. Gordon would read O'Connor's manuscripts and give her advice for the rest of O'Connor's life. She was O'Connor's most important literary mentor and most trusted advisor in matters artistic.

When she submitted the *Wise Blood* manuscript to Giroux in March, O'Connor's cover letter had expressed a wildly optimistic hope that the book would be published that fall. In November, with fall beginning to make its exit, O'Connor wrote to Giroux asking again for his patience while she finished working out the suggestions that Gordon had made. "I apologize for all this shilly-shallying," she said. "And keep on doing it." [24] On December 3, she finally sent Giroux the manuscript that would become the galley proofs of *Wise Blood*.

O'Connor may have been disappointed to find herself stuck at the farm with her mother, but her letters also reveal that she was keeping her eyes and ears open, observing local life and manners, collecting material that would find its way into her fiction. It would be almost two years before she wrote "The Displaced Person," a short story about a refugee family who come to work on a dairy farm and are destroyed by their inability to navigate the South's racial mores. But the story, it would seem, had its origins in December 1951. O'Connor wrote to the Fitzgeralds:

> My mamma is getting ready for what she hopes will be one of
> her blessings: a refugee family to arrive here Christmas night.
> She has to fix up and furnish a house for them, don't know

how many there will be or what nationality or occupation or nothing. She and Mrs. P., the dairyman's wife, have been making curtains for the windows out of flowered chicken-feed sacks. Regina was complaining that the green sacks wouldn't look so good in the same room where the pink ones were and Mrs. P. (who has no teeth on one side of her mouth) says in a very superior voice, "Do you think they'll know what colors even is?"[25]

O'Connor was always a visual writer. The attention to the physical details of the scene (the pink and green feed sacks, the missing teeth) and the complex yet ridiculous social dynamics (the ignorant woman's withering superiority) are hallmarks of both her fiction and her correspondence.

The beginning of 1952 brought the final preparations for the publication of *Wise Blood*. O'Connor made corrections to galleys. She got her author photos made. "They were all bad," she wrote to the Fitzgeralds. "The one I sent looked as if I had just bitten my grandmother and that this was one of my few pleasures, but all the rest were worse."[26] She settled on a dedication: "To Regina."

A few blurbs for the jacket copy trickled in. One of the most interesting came from Evelyn Waugh, the English Catholic author of *Brideshead Revisited*. "If this is really the unaided work of a young lady, it is a remarkable product." That one flabbergasted Regina, though not for the reasons it might have bothered Flannery. "My mother was vastly insulted," Flannery wrote to Robert Lowell. "She put the emphasis on *if* and *lady*. Does he suppose you're not a lady? she says. WHO is he?"[27]

In the end, Caroline Gordon's endorsement was the only one used on the book jacket. She compared O'Connor's terrifying vision of the modern world to Kafka's. That, too, elicited a reaction from Flannery's mother. Flannery wrote to the Fitzgeralds, "Regina is getting very literary. 'Who is this Kafka?' she says. 'People ask me.' A German Jew, I says, I think. He wrote a book about a man that turns into a roach. 'Well, I can't tell people *that*,' she says." [28]

O'Connor first saw a copy of *Wise Blood* in April before it was published on May 15, 1952. A bookseller in Milledgeville showed it to her. O'Connor hated the picture of herself, which took up the whole back of the jacket, looking, in her words, "like a refugee from deep thought."

As publication day approached, O'Connor had one more literary task to complete, this one assigned by her mother. She was "to write an introduction for Cousin Katie 'so she won't be shocked,' to be *pasted* on the inside of [Katie's copy of] the book. This piece has to be in the tone of the *Sacred Heart Messenger* and carry the burden of contemporary critical thought. I keep putting it off." [29]

O'Connor was on the cusp of literary greatness. In a month or two she would be one of the most talked-about writers in America. But in that matriarchal world where she lived and moved and had her being, the first concern was what the genteel Cousin Katie would think of a book so unorthodox, so seedy, so vulgar as *Wise Blood*.

6 | *WISE BLOOD*: 1952

When *Wise Blood* was published in May 1952, Flannery O'Connor was subjected to a round of parties in Milledgeville. She wrote to Robie Macauley, her friend from Iowa, who had a novel coming out, "I hope you won't have as much trouble about keeping people from having parties for you as I am having. Around here if you publish the number of whiskers on the local pigs, everybody has to give you a tea."[1]

To the Fitzgeralds she wrote, "An old dame that I abide with gritted teeth is having a luncheon for me on the 10th—only because she got to Regina before she got to me. Two others got to me before Regina and I squashed their plans to a pulp. I have to be very stealthy, all eyes and ears."[2]

The biggest of the parties was an "autograph party" on release day, held at the library of Georgia State College for Women. The event was attended by "throngs of guests" (one of whom was Cousin Katie from Savannah), according to the local paper. One of the most well-known photographs of O'Connor was taken at this event. She looks young and pretty and, by all appearances, healthy. And she is actually smiling—a rarity in her photographs, though not in real life.

Perhaps she was smiling to think of what all those proper Georgia ladies were going to think when they read her book. "It was very funny to see relics like Miss N. toting home a copy and to imagine it going on inside particular minds," she wrote to her old friend Betty Boyd Love.[3]

Indeed, Milledgevillians' politesse toward Regina's precocious girl belied a deep ambivalence regarding her accomplishment. Biographer Jean Cash quoted Milledgeville native Jay Lewis, who attended the party, on the locals' reaction to *Wise Blood*:

> Oh, they hated it; they were horrified by it. They couldn't imagine why a nice Southern girl would write such a book. . . . The average Milledgeville person would have seen them [O'Connor's characters] and would have thought this is how she sees us.[4]

Before *Wise Blood* released, O'Connor had some concerns about her family's reaction to the book. Those reservations, as it turned out, had some basis in reality. Cousin Katie took it hard, according to Brad Gooch, writing letters of apology to each of the priests to whom she had had copies sent before she had read it. It is rumored that she took to her bed for a week.[5] Gooch quotes a neighbor of Aunt Mary Cline who recalled the stately old woman sniffing, "I don't know where Mary Flannery met those people she wrote about, but it was certainly not in *my* house." As for Regina, Flannery reported, "She hasn't learned to love Mrs. Watts [the prostitute in *Wise Blood*]."[6]

There was not, however, any significant family fracture as the result of Mary Flannery's peculiar book. She had always been a free spirit, and though the family never learned to love Mrs. Watts and her ilk, they still loved the remarkable young woman who created them.

Four years later, O'Connor put things in perspective for a young writer named John Lynch who, apparently, had expressed some concern about his family's reaction to his work:

> I once had the feeling I would dig my mother's grave with my writing too, but I later discovered this was vanity on my part. They are hardier than we think. I also had an 83-year-old cousin who was fond of me and I was convinced that my novel was going to give her a stroke and that I was going to be pursued through life by the Furies. After she had read it, I waited for a letter announcing her decline but all I got was a curt note from her saying, "I do not like your book." She is now 88.[7]

After she made it through the *Wise Blood* parties, O'Connor would never endure another book release event in her honor. But the parties were scarcely over before she gave the first of the many author talks that she would deliver throughout the remainder of her life and career. These talks would be an important means by which O'Connor communicated her literary and theological vision. They also, as it turned out, afforded her an opportunity to be misunderstood right to her face.

Helen Green, a friend and former professor of O'Connor's at GSCW, invited her to speak to her class. The next day, O'Connor felt compelled to write Green a letter to clarify a few things that the students had misunderstood about her work:

> I was distressed yesterday to have some of your students tell me that I was a follower of Kafka and exhibited that pessimism

that had been going around with European intellectuals for the last fifty years but was just getting to the young people of this country. . . . Since my beliefs are a long way from Kafka I thought I'd better write you and see if I couldn't clear it up.[8]

If *Wise Blood* was Kafkaesque, she explained, it was only so in terms of technique: both wrote "a kind of fantasy rooted in the specific." But that commonality of technique did not, she insisted, point to a commonality in philosophy or belief. "My philosophical notions don't derive from Kierkegard (I can't even spell it), but from St. Thomas Aquinas. And I don't intend the tone of the book to be pessimistic. It is after all a story about redemption and if you admit redemption, you are no pessimist."[9]

The GSCW students' misunderstanding of *Wise Blood*—their misguided association of O'Connor's work with the existentialist philosophies of Kafka and Kierkegaard—would be the story of O'Connor's life when it came to academics and critics, especially early in her career. Her readers latched on to surface similarities in style (e.g., Kafka) or subject matter (e.g., the writers of the Southern Gothic tradition) as the key to understanding her work, and so missed the fact that she was putting twentieth-century literary techniques to ancient uses—which is to say, her debt to Kafka is nothing to her debt to Thomas Aquinas. "Everybody who has read *Wise Blood* thinks I'm a hillbilly nihilist," she complained a few years later, "whereas I would like to create the impression . . . that I am a hillbilly Thomist."[10]

It is often said that *Wise Blood* was released to mixed reviews. It may be more accurate to say that *Wise Blood* was misunderstood in different ways by different reviewers.

The review that appeared in *Commonweal*, a Catholic journal, is a microcosm of the critical reaction to *Wise Blood*. The reviewer admired, patronized, psychologized, congratulated himself for his cleverness, and contradicted himself throughout. *Wise Blood*, he wrote, "is a remarkably accomplished, remarkably precocious beginning," for a twenty-six-year-old novelist. Whatever gratification O'Connor received from this generous start must have been dulled, however, by the reviewer's description of the book as "a kind of Southern Baptist version of 'The Hound of Heaven.'" He was referring to the 1893 poem by Francis Thompson about God's relentless saving pursuit of the lost soul—not a bad comparison, but that descriptor "Southern Baptist" surely galled the devoutly Roman Catholic O'Connor. Though the setting and characters are Southern, no character in the book claims to be a Baptist.

The reviewer's blindness to the nuances of Christian experience would not, perhaps, be a significant thing, except that he plunged right into the middle of theological complexities. "Motes' rejection of Christ, or apparent rejection of Christ, can be explained simply. His childhood was fed on a crude evangelism which luridly associated Christ with sin."[11]

The idea that anything about the human soul "can be explained simply" would be news to Flannery O'Connor, who never went in for the Freudian reductionism that animates so much of the criticism written about her work. Having dismissed the possibility that Hazel Motes might actually be running from a God who actually pursues him—allowing only for the possibility that Hazel "can be explained simply"—the reviewer is left with the subhuman world he expected to find in a work of "the grotesque literature of Southern decadence."[12] He wrote, "There is more crude animalism in Taulkinham than in the fictional zoo of its outskirts. Nobody here is redeemed because there is no one to redeem."[13]

At the center of Flannery O'Connor's difficulties with the critics (or, rather, their difficulty with her) was the fact that critics' understanding of her fiction was filtered through their notions of Southern Gothic. In the critics' defense, a novel written by a Southerner and concerning itself with street preachers, lunatics, a prostitute, a teenage nymphomaniac, and a false prophet in a gorilla suit does deserve a place in "the grotesque literature of Southern degeneracy" that was being produced by such writers as Carson McCullers and Erskine Caldwell.[14]

But the degeneracy in O'Connor's stories is never the utter debasement of, say, the hookworm realism of Caldwell's *Tobacco Road* or the lurid voyeurism of McCullers's *Ballad of the Sad Café*. She does not, as the *New Republic* reviewer put it, "write of an insane world peopled by monsters and submen." In O'Connor's oeuvre even the most damaged sinners long for transcendence whether they know it or not, and transcendence makes its presence known at long last.

Caroline Gordon understood what the first reviewers of *Wise Blood* did not understand: that the freaks of O'Connor's fiction are human. "It is fashionable to write about freaks," Gordon wrote to O'Connor. "Truman Capote and his followers write about little else. It astonishes—and amuses me—to find a writer like you using what is roughly the same kind of subject matter." She continued, "You are giving us a terrifying picture of the modern world, so your book is full of freaks. They seem to me, however, normal people who have been maimed or crippled and your main characters, Sabbath, Enoch and Haze, are all going about their Father's business, as best they can."[15]

Perhaps the most important thing that sets O'Connor's work apart from that of her Southern Gothic contemporaries is the possibility that her lame will walk again and her maimed will be made whole.

Once *Wise Blood* was out of her hands, O'Connor turned her attention and energies to other creative endeavors. She took up oil painting—"mostly chickens and guineas and pheasants." Regina approved of her daughter's painting much more than she approved of her writing. Several of Flannery's paintings were hanging in the GSCW library on the day of her book release party.

In the spring of 1952, O'Connor started writing a story she called "The World Is Almost Rotten," which was published under the title "The Life You Save May Be Your Own." It is a complex story of a one-armed shyster's con game on a cagey, resourceful widow and her mentally retarded adult daughter living on a hardscrabble farm.

"The Life You Save" is O'Connor's first experiment with a dynamic that would drive six of the twenty-one short stories she wrote in the remainder of her career: the intense and conflicted relationship with a single mother and an adult son or daughter still living at home. The mothers, like Regina, are usually shrewd, sometimes naïve, and always overbearing. The sons and daughters are either debilitated or overeducated (which, in O'Connor's fictional world, is itself a kind of debility), or both. Joy-Hulga Hopewell of "Good Country People" has a PhD and a wooden leg; Asbury Fox of "The Enduring Chill" is both a third-rate playwright and a first-rate hypochondriac.

To the end of her life, Flannery O'Connor resisted autobiographical readings of her stories. But there is no mistaking the fact that "The Life You Save" represents a new willingness to use the facts of her situation as raw material for her fiction. If Aunt Mary wondered where Mary Flannery met the people she wrote about in *Wise Blood*, there would be no mistaking where she met many of the characters in the stories to come.

⁂

In June 1952, O'Connor finally returned to Connecticut for what was originally planned as a six-week visit to help out around the Fitzgerald house. Robert Fitzgerald was teaching for the summer at the Indiana School of Letters, and Sally was pregnant with their fifth child. O'Connor brought three live ducks to the Fitzgerald children, having smuggled them on the airplane.

The Fitzgerald house was more chaotic than usual that summer. On top of the fact that Robert was away, the four Fitzgerald children were joined for the second half of O'Connor's visit, by Mary Loretta, a twelve-year-old African American girl from New York City. She was there through the Fresh Air Fund, which gave inner-city children the opportunity to enjoy a summer vacation with a host family. The children's nanny, a Slovenian refugee named Maria, had never seen a black person and reacted very badly to Mary Loretta. Mary Loretta, by O'Connor's account, was no angel, but any misbehavior on her part was eclipsed by Maria's "scowls, mutterings, and tantrums of varying intensity, in Slovenian."[16] Sally Fitzgerald grew concerned that the drama and disorder might cause her to miscarry.

In the midst of this chaos, O'Connor learned for certain what she suspected already but had never heard spoken aloud: she suffered from lupus. Sally Fitzgerald broke the news to her while they were driving back from running errands in town. Brad Gooch tells the story, drawing on an interview conducted with Sally Fitzgerald by the documentary filmmaker Christopher O'Hare.

She had made up her mind, following much inner struggle, that Flannery should finally know the true nature of her illness. At that instant, Flannery happened to mention her arthritis. "Flannery, you don't have arthritis," Sally said quickly. "You have lupus." Reacting to the sudden revelation, Flannery slowly moved her arm from the car door down into her lap, her hand visibly trembling. . . . "Well, that's not good news," Flannery said, after a few silent, charged moments. "But I can't thank you enough for telling me. . . . I thought I had lupus, and I thought I was going crazy. I'd a lot rather be sick than crazy."[17]

As if in confirmation of the news, O'Connor caught a virus at the Fitzgeralds' house, requiring her to cut her visit short by a week. Arriving in Atlanta, she went straight to an appointment at Dr. Merrill's office. Seventeen months after first diagnosing her disease, Merrill finally told O'Connor that she had lupus. He further told her that the virus she caught in Connecticut had reawakened the dormant disease.

"I now know that it is lupus and am very glad to so know," O'Connor wrote to Robert Fitzgerald. "[Dr. Merrill] increased my dose but doesn't think I will have any trouble."[18] He was wrong on that last count. Later in the summer, O'Connor wrote to Sally Fitzgerald, who was on bed rest, "Greetings from my bed of affliction to yourn. I have been on it two weeks with the fevers & etceteras and am like to be two more."[19] In the event, she spent six weeks in bed.

If O'Connor had hoped that her lengthy visit with the Fitzgeralds was a test run for a permanent move away from Milledgeville, that hope was dashed. It now seemed obvious that Flannery O'Connor wouldn't be leaving the farm. Shortly after her meeting with Dr. Merrill, she wrote a note to Elizabeth McKee that began, simply,

I am now back in Georgia.[20]

Full stop. New paragraph. New start.

O'Connor wrote to ask Sally Fitzgerald to ship back two suit-cases of her things that she had left in December 1950 when she first came down with her disease. It had been an act of optimism, leaving her things in Connecticut against her eventual return, but now it was time to get on with her life in Milledgeville.

ஃ

For O'Connor, one of the great benefits of life in Milledgeville was the opportunity to observe and record the manners of the locals, who provided rich fodder for her fiction. Many of her observations were filtered through her mother, who obviously had an ear for anecdote herself. She especially enjoyed the new family of farmhands who moved to Andalusia that summer:

My mama says she has never read *Tobacco Road* but she thinks it's moved in. I don't know how long they will be with us but I am enjoying it while it lasts, and I aim to give my gret reading audiance a shot of some of the details sometime. Every time Regina brings in some new information, our educ. is broad-ened considerably.[21]

The family didn't last to the end of the year, "but I learned a lot while they were here," O'Connor said.

The locals, evidently, were inspiring. In spite of her health problems, O'Connor was productive in the second half of the year. After coming home from Connecticut, she completed "The Life You Save May Be Your Own," wrote "A Late Encounter with the Enemy" (inspired by an article she read in the local paper) and "The River," while beginning a second novel, which, after years of struggle, would finally become *The Violent Bear It Away*.

That second half of the year also brought more public successes. "Late Encounter" was accepted almost immediately at *Harper's Bazaar*. In the fall she also received an admiring letter from John Crowe Ransom, editor of the *Kenyon Review*. Having first become familiar with O'Connor's work when at the Iowa Writers' Workshop, he was a fan of *Wise Blood*. He encouraged O'Connor to apply for the *Kenyon Review* fellowship, a $2,000 prize funded by the Rockefellers.

In December, O'Connor learned that she had won the fellowship. "I reckon most of this money will go to blood and ACTH and books, with a few sideline researches into the ways of the vulgar," she wrote. The prize also had the added benefit of raising her work in the esteem of her mother:

> My mamma is getting a big bang out of notifying all the kin
> who didn't like the book that the Rockerfeller Foundation,
> etc. etc.—this very casual like on the back of Christmas cards.
> Money talks, she says, and the name of Rockerfeller don't
> hurt a bit.[22]

Around the same time, Flannery O'Connor ordered the first of the peafowl that would become the most familiar symbol of

Andalusia and her life there. For many years she had longed to add peacocks to her collection of chickens and ducks and guineas and pheasants. The realization that she was at Andalusia to stay brought the consolation, at least, that she would finally be able to fulfill that dream.

For the practical and fastidious Regina, peafowl were not an obvious fit for Andalusia. Flannery told the story in "The King of the Birds," her 1961 piece for *Holiday* magazine.

"Don't those things eat flowers?" [Regina] asked.

"They'll eat Startena [Purina's game bird feed] like the rest of them," I said.[23]

Later in the same piece, O'Connor quipped,

I was correct that my peachickens would all eat Startena; they also eat everything else. Particularly they eat flowers. My mother's fears were all borne out. Peacocks not only eat flowers, they eat them systematically, beginning at the head of a row and going down it. If they are not hungry, they will pick the flower anyway, if it is attractive, and let it drop.[24]

When the peafowl first arrived by train from Florida, it was the beginning of a lifelong love for O'Connor, though, in her telling, it was an unrequited love, since a peacock shows scant regard for any human being who isn't in the act of feeding it. "As soon as the birds were out of the crate, I sat down on it and began to look at them. I have been looking at them ever since, from one station or another, and always with the same awe as on that first occasion."[25]

Into her mundane world, O'Connor imported the bird of Hera, Zeus's wife. Eventually, dozens of them preened and strutted on Middle Georgia's red clay. For all their mess and trouble and greed and vanity, they offered a glimpse of the heavenlies.

> When it suits him, the peacock will face you. Then you will see in a green-bronze arch around him a galaxy of gazing, haloed suns. This is the moment when most people are silent.
>
> "Amen! Amen!" an old Negro woman once cried when this happened, and I have heard many similar remarks at this moment that show the inadequacy of human speech. Some people whistle; a few, for once, are silent.[26]

Flannery O'Connor's peacocks, like her fiction, are a reminder that the rural South is as good a place as any for Transcendence to break through and reveal itself to the human gaze.

7 | "I SEEM TO ATTRACT THE LUNATIC FRINGE": 1953–1954

"Money talks," Regina said when she learned that her daughter had won the *Kenyon Review* fellowship. Money certainly talked to the family. "My kinfolks think I am a commercial writer now and really they are proud of me,"[1] O'Connor wrote.

She seemed a little embarrassed by the fact that "A Late Encounter with the Enemy" was being published in a magazine as popular as *Harper's Bazaar*. "Nobody sees things in those magazines except the ladies that go to the beauty parlors,"[2] she told Robert and Elizabeth Lowell. But there were a lot more old ladies in beauty parlors than there were people reading the literary quarterlies where O'Connor's stories were usually published. In the 1950s, the circulation of *Harper's Bazaar* was close to 300,000. The *Kenyon Review*, by contrast, boasted about 2,000 readers.

In O'Connor's literary world, of course, it was true enough that "nobody" read *Harper's Bazaar*. But in her other world, the one where she lived bodily, it was a triumph. If she wasn't a household name in Georgia, she at least was beginning to experience a certain fame. She told the Fitzgeralds, "My uncle Louis is always bringing me a message from somebody at [his company] who has read *Wise Blood*. The last was: ask her why she don't write about some nice people. Louis says, I told them you wrote what *paid*."[3]

O'Connor didn't have to go far to continue her researches into the ways of the vulgar. When her uncle Louis wasn't around, she could observe the new dairyman's family—the most delightfully vulgar yet:

> Old man P. [the previous dairyman] looked like he might have had an ancestor back a couple of centuries ago who was at least a decayed gentleman (he wouldn't wear overalls; only khaki) but these . . . look like they've been joined up with the human race for only a couple of months now. Mrs. W. says she went to school for one day and didn't loin nothin and ain't went back. She has four children and I thought she was one of them. The oldest girl is 14 with a mouth full of snuff.[4]

O'Connor's health was still bad at the beginning of 1954. Her hair was thin on top, and her face had swollen up again. "I think that this is going to be permanent," she said in January 1953. Looking on the bright side as usual, she pointed out that at least knowing that her disease was lupus enabled her to take better care of herself. She stayed out of the sun and avoided exercise. She wrote in March, "I have enough energy to write with and as that is all I have any business doing anyhow, I can with one eye squinted take it all as a blessing. What you have to measure out, you come to observe closer, or so I tell myself."[5]

Indeed, no matter what her physical state, she cherished the time given her. And it is possible to believe that she did manage to see her health issues as a blessing. It is possible that in some ways her debility spurred her creative production rather than curtailed it. She carefully stewarded the energy she had, seizing every minute she could to do the work she felt called to do.

O'Connor's habits were extremely regular. Prayers before sunup. Mass at 7:15. A morning of writing. An afternoon of reading correspondence and responding to it, receiving visitors, and looking at peafowl. In the evenings she read—philosophy, theology, fiction, criticism. Her letters (and even more so, the 120 reviews she wrote for two diocesan newspapers) demonstrate how deeply she engaged the books she read.

Each day for the "hillbilly Thomist" ended with twenty minutes' reading in Thomas Aquinas's *Summa Theologica*—a daily brushup on the fundamentals of her faith.

> If my mother were to come in during this process and say, "Turn off that light. It's late," I with lifted finger and broad bland beatific expression would reply, "On the contrary, I answer that the light, being eternal and limitless, cannot be turned off. Shut your eyes," or some such thing.[6]

It's a classic O'Connor moment. The practical, solicitous mother issues an order. The witty, overeducated daughter smarts off piously.

O'Connor was almost as faithful to her letter writing as she was to her fiction writing. Correspondence had its own slot in the daily schedule. Letters were her most important connection to the world beyond her circumscribed life in Milledgeville. The O'Connors didn't have a telephone until 1956; anyone wishing to get a message to Flannery or Regina had to call Aunt Mary at the Cline mansion in town. But Aunt Mary wasn't very reliable. "She lives in the upper regions of reality and seldom remembers to give any messages that come,"[7] said O'Connor.

Letters, for O'Connor, were friendship by other means. She received news and gave it, she explained herself, she argued, she gave advice, she encouraged, she occasionally scolded. Her closest friends were people whom she almost never saw, but whom she invited to share in her inner life through letters.

As her writing gained popularity, she got more and more notes from strangers, many of whom she answered with thoughtful letters. A good number of the letters came "from people I might have created," she said. A Jimmie Crum of Los Angeles wrote to ask her what became of the man in the gorilla suit in *Wise Blood* and asked for a photograph of the author that he could hang in his office. Two theology students wrote to tell her that she was their "pin-up girl" ("the grimmest distinction yet"). One letter came from "a real West Virginia mountineer to his writer-friend" who wrote, "I have a serious heart and blood vessel condition, don't want a penny or pity but sure do like the way you form words—sinsationally, wow, ha ha."[8] O'Connor had always been a collector of the absurd; she read these letters with relish. Nevertheless, she wrote, "I wish somebody real intelligent would write me sometime but I seem to attract the lunatic fringe."[9]

Every now and then, O'Connor initiated a correspondence with a reader. The fall 1952 issue of *Shenandoah Quarterly* featured a review of *Wise Blood* that was unlike the other reviews the book had received. The review compared *Wise Blood* to Erskine Caldwell's *Tobacco Road* on the one hand and Faulkner's *As I Lay Dying* on the other. In the reviewer's description, Caldwell was "no artist and only a dull pornographer," reducing his white-trash characters to animals through one indignity after another. Any talk of religion in *Tobacco Road*, he wrote, is strictly on the surface and has nothing to do with any spiritual realm, which has been excluded from the book's universe. *As I Lay Dying*, on the other hand, does acknowledge that there is a deeper hunger than the clay-eating hunger of *Tobacco Road*; its characters look to religion of a sort—specifically, Addie's funeral rites—to take the edge off that hunger. But they aren't seeking salvation, and when the funeral is over, they are back to their naturalistic lives.

But *Wise Blood*, the reviewer argued, is another thing entirely:

> *Wise Blood* is not about belly hunger, nor religious nostalgia, but about the persistent craving of the soul. It is not about a man whose religious allegiance is a name for a shiftlessness and fatalism that make him degenerate in poverty and bestial before hunger, nor about a family of rustics who sink in naturalistic anonymity when the religious elevation of their burial rite is over. It is about man's inescapable need of his fearful, if blind, search for salvation.[10]

At last, a reviewer was reading *Wise Blood* on its own terms and so understood what O'Connor was trying to do. The reviewer was Brainard Cheney of Nashville, Tennessee. O'Connor was so impressed with the review that she wrote Caroline Gordon—who had lived for many years in Nashville with her husband, Allen Tate, and "appears to know everybody who ever wrote anything in Tennessee"—to ask if she knew Cheney. Gordon did know him, and she sent O'Connor his address.

The next day O'Connor wrote a letter to Cheney to tell him how much she appreciated the review of her much-misunderstood book.

There have not been many good ones. I've been surprised again and again to learn what a tough character I must be to have produced a work so lacking in what one lady called "love." The love of God doesn't count or else I didn't make it recognizable. So many reviewers too thought it was just another dirty book and enjoyed it for that reason.[11]

When Cheney wrote back, he confessed that he was "the perfect set-up" for her story. He was a brand-new convert to Catholicism ("ex-Protestant, ex-agnostic"). Caroline Gordon, he said, was not only his literary godmother but his godmother in the church. He was a novelist and playwright. He was also a native of Lumber City, Georgia, less than a hundred miles south of Milledgeville.

Cheney asked permission to "pursue this introduction into acquaintance."[12] And thus began another vital friendship in Flannery O'Connor's life. Brainard and Francis Cheney lived outside Nashville in the town of Smyrna, in a big nineteenth-century brick house they called Cold Chimneys. Brainard, besides being a novelist, was a journalist and the communications director for the governor of Tennessee. Francis, or Fanny, was a well-known librarian at Peabody College, which is now a school within Vanderbilt University. Cold Chimneys was a hub of literary culture in Nashville; while a student at Vanderbilt, Brainard had become friends with many of the "Fugitive" writers, including John Crowe Ransom, Robert Penn Warren, Cleanth Brooks, and Andrew Lytle. His house was a frequent gathering place for the "Nashville literati" at a time when Nashville was an important center of American letters. Allen and Caroline Gordon Tate were frequent visitors to Cold Chimneys. Flannery O'Connor would soon join the circle.

Shenandoah, the same quarterly that published Cheney's review, published O'Connor's "A Stroke of Good Fortune" in the spring 1953 issue. Originally titled "Woman on the Stairs," it began as part of *Wise Blood*. Ruby Hill, the story's central character, was Hazel Motes's sister in her first incarnation. She disappeared from the novel early in the writing process but reappears here, a country girl trying to put her hardscrabble past behind her and secure a more modern and middle-class life in the city—or, ideally, in the suburbs. She fears nothing so much as getting pregnant, believing that bearing and raising a child will suck the vitality out of her, just as it had her mother, who bore eight children and "had got deader with every one of them." A palm reader promised Ruby that a long illness would bring her a "stroke of good fortune." Ruby's world shatters when she realizes that she is pregnant: the palm reader's stroke of good fortune is a baby.

The story "is, in its way, Catholic," O'Connor wrote, "being about the rejection of life at the source."[13] But she was not satisfied with the story. It was too much of a farce, she believed, to bear such weight as that. At the same time, she was writing another story that started out as farce before turning suddenly, almost without warning, into something much grimmer. "A Good Man Is Hard to Find" is still O'Connor's most widely anthologized and best-known story. It begins with the most commonplace of circumstances: a family driving from Atlanta to Florida—bratty children, exasperated parents, and a dotty grandmother who speaks almost exclusively in clichés. They get off the highway, get turned around, and get murdered by escaped convicts led by the serial killer known as the Misfit.

It is a troubling story. The grandmother at its center is shallow and hypocritical and annoying and not the sort of person anyone would relish a road trip with. But her punishment—if that's what her murder is—seems all out of proportion to her slight crimes. As Flannery O'Connor herself observed, everybody has a grandmother or great-aunt very much like her. It is a hard thing to see her face-to-face with such evil and violence as the Misfit's.

"With the serious writer," O'Connor wrote, "violence is never an end in itself. It is the extreme situation that best reveals what we are essentially, and I believe that these are times when writers are more interested in what we are essentially than in the tenor of our daily lives." Which helps explains why a story that looks at first like a brilliantly rendered but lightweight slice of daily life takes such a turn as this one does.

> I have found that violence is strangely capable of returning my characters to reality and preparing them to accept their moment of grace. Their heads are so hard that almost nothing else will do the work. This idea, that reality is something to which we must be returned at considerable cost, is one which is seldom understood by the casual reader, but it is one which is implicit in the Christian view of the world.[14]

For the grandmother, the realization that she was somehow kin to the Misfit was more valuable to her than her earthly life, even if she didn't understand that it was. In the last of her many efforts to manipulate others, the grandmother tells the Misfit that he is a good man. But he isn't. His heart is black. Still, the grandmother's realization that she is connected to him is a crack through which grace can flow into her life (and flow outward too, though the Misfit rejects such grace with a gunshot).

As it turns out, the comic element in "A Good Man Is Hard to Find," and all of Flannery O'Connor's stories, is not incongruous with either the violence or the spiritual element that it rubs against. "In general the Devil can always be a subject for my kind of comedy one way or another," O'Connor wrote. "I suppose this is because he is always accomplishing ends other than his own."[15]

❧

Sometimes people just showed up at Andalusia to meet the author. Since there was no telephone, there was usually no warning. In late April 1953, Regina opened the door to an unusual stranger who had made his way up the long drive from Highway 441. He was a tall, blond Dane—a Harcourt textbook salesman named Erik Langkjaer. He had been making sales calls at Georgia State College for Women, where he met Helen Green, O'Connor's friend and former professor. Green encouraged the literate, intelligent Langkjaer to pay a visit to O'Connor—one of his company's authors—before leaving town.

Regina left the two young people alone to talk. Their conversation went well beyond small talk. They talked philosophy and theology and politics. They spoke of Dorothy Day, the Catholic activist who was a leader in social justice issues and whom Langkjaer had met through an aunt. O'Connor was ambivalent toward Day, but Langkjaer, it seems, admired her even less. "He couldn't see he said why she fed endless lines of endless bums for whom there was no hope, she'd never see any results from that, said he."[16]

Though he was a textbook salesman, Langkjaer brought an air of cosmopolitanism to Andalusia. He had survived both the divorce of his parents and the Nazi occupation of Denmark.

He came to America after the war to join his mother, who had immigrated to New York in 1939. He studied political science at Princeton, then philosophy at Fordham University, a Jesuit school, where he also taught German. At Fordham he was befriended by Father William Lynch, whose writings helped shape O'Connor's aesthetics. But Langkjaer, while he had an affinity for Catholicism, simply didn't believe, and the prospect of teaching philosophy in Catholic colleges—the obvious path forward—caused him considerable mental anguish. Father Lynch encouraged him to leave Fordham and seek another path.[17]

So Langkjaer found himself selling textbooks across the South. He and O'Connor formed an instant bond of friendship. He frequently came to Andalusia on weekends through the rest of 1953 and into 1954. He and O'Connor had long talks on the porch and took long walks through the fields and went on long car rides through the countryside.

∞

In the summer of 1953, O'Connor was well enough to travel. Having received a visit from the Cheneys in June, she reciprocated by flying to Nashville for a weekend in late July or August. In August she visited the Fitzgeralds for three weeks that were considerably less eventful than her previous visit. It was her last visit before the Fitzgeralds moved to Italy. For the remainder of O'Connor's life, the Fitzgeralds would not live in the United States.

Shortly after Flannery's return from Connecticut, the "displaced persons" Regina had begun preparing for a year and a half earlier finally arrived. Coming from Poland by way of West Germany, the Matysiaks were among the millions of Eastern Europeans left homeless after World War II. From Displaced

Persons' camps (or DP camps) in Europe, these families scattered throughout the world. A few ended up in Middle Georgia as farm laborers, but, according to O'Connor, "usually the families that have been got around here for dairy work turned out to be . . . shoemakers and have headed for Chicago just as soon as they could save the money. For which they can't be blamed."[18]

The Matysiaks were diligent workers, but they were very much outsiders in Milledgeville. At Andalusia they were dropped into a complicated dynamic of race and class that was as foreign to them as they were to it. Black and white was one thing, but then there were the social differences between the O'Connors who owned the place and the white dairyman's family, the Stevenses. It was Mrs. Stevens who remarked of the last family of DPs (who never arrived), "Do they even know what colors is?"

Those complexities became the basis of O'Connor's story "The Displaced Person," which she wrote in the fall of 1953. In this story, a family of European refugees arrives at a dairy farm and, by their diligent attention to their work, utterly upset the social order on the farm, where the grading had always been done on a very generous curve. The turning point of the story comes when the displaced person suggests that one of the black farmhands marry his cousin in order to get her out of the DP camp in Europe. This breaking of racial taboo has tragic results; in the end, everyone in the story is displaced.

No such tragedy took place at Andalusia, though there was a certain amount of drama. The Matysiaks left Andalusia in 1954 but came back two years later. Even now, there are still Matysiaks in Milledgeville.

The second half of 1953 was a time of great productivity for O'Connor. Besides writing "The Displaced Person," she also wrote "A Circle in the Fire" and "A Temple of the Holy Ghost."

"We have a girls' college here too," O'Connor once wrote of Milledgeville, "but the lacy atmosphere is fortunately destroyed by a reformatory, an insane asylum, and a military school."[19] The boys' reformatory, in fact, was quite close to Andalusia, and escaped boys sometimes fled in the O'Connors' direction. She wrote to a friend,

> We are busy being host to the junior underworld. The reformatory is about a mile away and the lads escape this time of year. Last week we had six one day, one the next, and two the next. They track them down through the woods with other reformatory boys. We would much prefer that they use dogs.[20]

Those roaming delinquents make their way into "A Circle in the Fire." Three teenage boys show up at a farm that looks very much like Andalusia. It is clear from the start that they are bent on a destructiveness that serves no purpose. Part of the action in the story is observed through the eyes of a preadolescent girl, the daughter of the widow who runs the farm; she is both fascinated and terrified by the boys. She watches from her hiding places, trying to understand what the boys are about, but she doesn't have the wherewithal to make sense of what she is seeing.

"A Temple of the Holy Ghost" is also told from the point of view of a girl on the front edge of adolescence. An intellectually precocious twelve-year-old discovers just how young she is when two fourteen-year-old, boy-crazy cousins come to visit. The mysteries of sexuality, already impenetrable to the girl, grow even more fearful when her cousins come home from a carnival freak show with the story of a hermaphrodite.

It is a dangerous thing to attempt to deduce an author's psychology from her fiction. Nevertheless, it is hard not to read the girls in "A Circle in the Fire" and "A Temple of the Holy Ghost" in terms of O'Connor's relationship with Erik Langkjaer. In her entire body of work, these are the only two stories that employ a young girl's point of view.[21] O'Connor, who had resolved not to get any older than twelve, had very little romantic experience. But in her mind at least, she was on the threshold of a mature romantic relationship. She was, in other words, uniquely attuned to the fears, the doubts, and the incomprehension of a pubescent girl just beginning to awaken to her own sexuality.

The latter part of 1953 brought a new development in O'Connor's health. She started to limp due to a new pain in her hip. Her doctors assured her that it was not directly related to lupus but instead was rheumatism. She wrote to a friend, "It galls me to have supported the lupus for four years and then to be crippled with rheumatism (a vulgar disease at best) of the hip."[22] She complained that she wasn't crippled enough for a cane but too crippled to walk straight, "so that I give the appearance of merely being a little drunk all the time."

Her debility did not help her love life. She had fallen in love with Erik Langkjaer; years later she referred to him as someone she "used to go with." But Langkjaer wasn't interested. Reflecting long afterward on his relationship with O'Connor, he wrote, "Battling with lupus had somewhat deformed her features and I was probably not mature enough to seriously consider the prospect of marriage."[23]

In May 1954, Langkjaer picked up O'Connor in his car and took her for a drive in the country. He told her that he was going back to Denmark for the summer. Mark Bosco tells the story of that drive, based on interviews with Langkjaer:

> He turned off to the side of a country road and stopped the
> motor. He pulled Flannery over to himself and she did not, he

says, draw away. Only two or three kisses were exchanged but the effect on Erik was startling. He felt not only her evident lack of experience; he felt suddenly very frightened by her illness, possibly realizing for the first time how ill she was.[24]

O'Connor surely found it confusing for a man to kiss her for the first time immediately after telling her that he would be going away.

While Langkjaer was in Europe, O'Connor wrote to him regularly. In her letters to him, there is a tenderness that does not appear anywhere else in her correspondence. "I haven't seen any dirt roads since you left and I miss you," she wrote.

Her letters to Langkjaer are as whip-smart and literary and philosophical and theological as her other letters, but they are punctuated by endearments that are heartbreaking to read. "Dear, dear Erik"—she wrote when he told her he would be staying in Copenhagen for six months rather than just for the summer— "You are wildly and wonderfully original and I would probably think you even more so if I didn't still hope you will come back from that awful place."[25]

She confided that she called one of her baby peachickens Erik in private. She wrote at length of her hope that he would experience a religious conversion. But the letters from Langkjaer came less often—a fact that was not lost on Regina O'Connor. "Write me an unintelligible postcard please so I will have an excuse to write you a letter," Flannery wrote. "My mother don't think it is proper for me to send mail when I don't receive it."

"Write me because I so want to hear," she wrote in a later letter. In a handwritten postscript to her letter, she added, "I feel like if you were here we could talk about a million years without stopping."[26]

But she may not have wanted to hear. Shortly after sending that letter, O'Connor finally received a letter from Langkjaer. It brought her the news that he was getting married to a woman he had met in Copenhagen. She would never see him again.

8 | *A GOOD MAN IS HARD TO FIND*: 1954–1955

It took Flannery O'Connor five years to finish *Wise Blood.* Her second novel wasn't coming along any faster. She suggested that the burst of productivity in 1953 and 1954 that resulted in "A Good Man Is Hard to Find," "A Circle in the Fire," "A Temple of the Holy Ghost," and "The Displaced Person" was in part an effort to avoid writing her novel. "The agony is over quicker" with a short story, she said.[1]

In late 1953, O'Connor started gathering her short stories for the collection that would come out in 1955 as *A Good Man Is Hard to Find and Other Short Stories.* In the spring of 1954, she started on a new story she called "The Artificial Nigger." The title refers to the black jockey statuary that used to be common on lawns in white neighborhoods in the South. The story first started taking shape while driving in the countryside on a cow-buying venture when Regina asked directions. She couldn't miss the house, she was told, because "it was the only house in town with an artificial nigger." Besides being struck with the phrase itself, O'Connor saw it as "a terrible symbol of what the South has done to itself."[2]

"The Artificial Nigger" is the story of a backwoodsman named Mr. Head and his insufferable grandson Nelson. Though he was raised in the country by his grandfather and remembers nothing else, Nelson prides himself on having been born in Atlanta. Mr. Head takes the boy to Atlanta for the sole purpose of demonstrating that the city is "no kind of place" for people like them. The old man assumes that once Nelson sees that his birthplace is full of black people, he won't be so arrogant. When Mr. Head and Nelson get lost and wander into a black neighborhood, they both feel that they are beyond their depth. In a moment of fear and danger, when Nelson finally understands how much he needs his grandfather, Mr. Head denies that he even knows the boy. And so the old man is forced to come face-to-face with his moral bankruptcy—and the possibility of grace in spite of it. The story's penultimate paragraph spells out O'Connor's theological purposes more clearly than usual:

> He stood appalled, judging himself with the thoroughness of God, while the action of mercy covered his pride like a flame and consumed it. He had never thought himself a great sinner before but he saw now that his true depravity had been hidden from him lest it cause him despair. He realized that he was forgiven for sins from the beginning of time. . . . He saw that no sin was too monstrous to claim as his own, and since God loved in proportion as He forgave, he felt ready at that instant to enter Paradise.[3]

O'Connor considered "The Articifial Nigger" to be the best thing she would ever write. She spent two or three months on the story, wrestling with the best way to present fictionally "an apparent action of grace."

"What I had in mind to suggest with the artificial nigger," she wrote, "was the redemptive quality of the Negro's suffering for us all."[4] Readers have been troubled, however, by the fact that Mr. Head's redemption does not involve any softening of his bigoted attitudes. It never seems to dawn on Mr. Head—though it is clear enough to the reader—that the black people he encounters are more humane than he is. When Mr. Head and Nelson reconcile, they reconcile over a racist joke. Whatever has changed in the two by the end of the story, it is not their bigotry. It is yet another strange expression of grace— one that shows, even as it does its work, how desperately its recipients need it.

John Crowe Ransom accepted "The Artificial Nigger" for the *Kenyon Review*. He objected to the title, but O'Connor stood firm. "The story as a whole is much more damaging to white folks' sensibilities than to black," she wrote to Ransom.[5] She fully intended for the title to be shocking and offensive. The story was published—with its original title—in the spring 1955 issue of the *Kenyon Review*.

On November 15, 1954, O'Connor sent Robert Giroux a full manuscript of her short story collection. Within a month, however, she was changing her mind. On the advice of Caroline Gordon, who still read and commented on everything she wrote, O'Connor had revised and expanded "The Artificial Nigger." The expansion put the book over its allotted page limit. Giroux recommended cutting either "An Afternoon in the Woods" (a revision of "The Turkey," from O'Connor's master's thesis) or "A Stroke of Good Fortune" to make room for the expansions. O'Connor suggested that both be removed.

During the winter of 1955, the rheumatism in O'Connor's hip got worse. She started walking with a cane. Dr. Merrill assured her that the increased pain was not an indication that her lupus was flaring up again, but was strictly rheumatism. After the long deception following her original diagnosis, O'Connor was understandably reluctant to take the doctor at his word. "I would not believe it except that the dose of ACTH has not been increased. Besides which I now feel it makes very little difference what you call it."[6] By the end of March she would report to Giroux that she had put away the cane. But she would deal with severe hip pain for the rest of her life, going from cane to crutches with only the briefest periods of walking unaided.

In February, O'Connor sat down and pounded out a new story in three days—an unheard-of pace for her. "Good Country People" is the story of Joy-Hulga Hopewell, an overeducated, unemployed, and intellectually prideful young woman who lives with her widowed mother on the family farm. She has a wooden leg, having lost her leg in a shooting accident, and she has dedicated herself to being as ugly, inside and out, as she can possibly be—an expression of her intellectual nihilism. The name Hulga is her invention, chosen for its ugliness to displace the name Joy that her mother had given her: Joy.

When a young Bible salesman shows up, Joy-Hulga gets it in her head to seduce the boy. She imagines it will be easy. She further imagines that she—being free from the constraints of conventional morality—will have to help the poor Bible salesman deal with the guilt that would inevitably result from the loss of his virginity:

True genius can get an idea across even to an inferior mind.
She imagined that she took his remorse in hand and changed it

into a deeper understanding of life. She took all his shame away and turned it into something useful.[7]

In the end, however, it is the Bible salesman who gains the upper hand. He maneuvers her to the hayloft for the "seduction," and, having convinced her to take off her wooden leg, he steals it and leaves her alone in the hayloft. Just before disappearing down the ladder, he mocks Hulga in her helplessness: "'I'll tell you another thing, Hulga,' he said, using the name as if he didn't think much of it, 'you ain't so smart. I been believing in nothing since I was born!'"[8]

It is worth noting that O'Connor was writing this story even as she was writing unanswered letter after unanswered letter to Erik Langkjaer, the traveling book salesman who had raised her romantic hopes for perhaps the first time, then left her on the farm.

As usual, O'Connor sent "Good Country People" to Caroline Gordon. Gordon and her husband, Allen Tate, thought it was the best thing O'Connor had ever written. On February 26, scarcely three months before her short story collection was scheduled to release, she wrote her editor again asking for a major change to the book. "It is really a story that would set the whole collection on its feet," she wrote.[9] And it would be the only story in the collection that had never appeared anywhere else. Upon reading the story, Giroux agreed that "Good Country People" should be included in the collection. He cut "An Afternoon in the Woods" to make room (though he kept "A Stroke of Good Fortune").

As publication day approached for *A Good Man Is Hard to Find*, O'Connor spent more of her time speaking publically. At the end of March, she attended a writer's conference in Greensboro, North Carolina. "The panel was the worst as I never can think of anything to say about a story and the conferences were high comedy," she wrote to her friend Robie Macauley. "I had one with a bearded intellectual delinquent from Kenyon who wouldn't be convinced that he hadn't written a story, and the rest with girls writing about life in the dormitory."[10] She often found herself in the position of teaching young writers and students in a conference or seminar setting, the more so as time went on. But she didn't have much patience for such people. "Anything I can't stand it's a young writer or intellectual," she once wrote. But the colleges paid her good money for it. And though possessed of a large dairy farm, Regional and her daughter needed the cash.

She also found herself speaking at more and more local ladies' clubs and literary circles, which were a rich source of material for her letters. When the Macon Writers' Club held a breakfast in her honor on April 23, 1955, one woman informed her that she was there on an auspicious day: the birthday of William Shakespeare, Harry Stillwell Edwards, and Shirley Temple. That mix of literary culture and low popular culture—Shakespeare and Shirley Temple—was precisely to O'Connor's taste. She always looked on these events with an ironic eye. "I have been wasting my time all these years writing," she told a friend. "My talent lies in a kind of intellectual vaudeville. I leave them not knowing exactly what I have said, but feeling that they have been inspired. . . . My mother thinks this is very fine and likely to *broaden* me; she finds me very narrow in my outlook."[11]

O'Connor actively cultivated her interest in low culture, and especially her interest in the varieties of Protestantism that swirled around her in the mass media. She never missed Dr. Frank Crane, an advice columnist whom she described as "an odd mixture of fundamentalism (against the grape), psychology, business administration and Dale Carnegie."[12] Appearing on the same page as the comics in the *Atlanta Constitution*, he was a prophet of positive thinking, regularly reporting success stories of people who smile and compliment others. O'Connor jokingly called him her "favorite Protestant theologian."[13]

In one sense, however, O'Connor was serious when she spoke of Dr. Crane as a Protestant theologian. From where she sat, mainstream American Protestantism was being shaped more and more by his brand of feel-good theology. Speaking of evangelist Ruth Plunkett she said, "Plunkett is really real modern when you come down to it—'pray and your food will taste better' is just another version of 'Grace before meals is an aid to digestion' which is what religion is coming to in some parts."[14]

O'Connor looked upon the Dr. Cranes and Ruth Plunketts of the world with amused detachment. But her interest in fundamentalists and other religious outliers, as embodied in her fiction, is another thing altogether. Unmoored from dogma, mainstream Protestantism was liable to drift anywhere, in O'Connor's view of things. But a fundamentalist, even if O'Connor believed him to be wrong, at least had a sense of doctrinal and scriptural authority that provided common ground with O'Connor and other Catholics. According to O'Connor's formulation,

> The Catholic finds it easier to understand the atheist than the Protestant, but easier to love the Protestant than the atheist. The fact is though now that the fundamentalist Protestants, as far as doctrine goes, are closer to their traditional enemy, the Church of Rome, than they are to the advanced elements in Protestantism.[15]

O'Connor did not populate her stories with religious crazies for the purpose of mocking them. Though modernists are mocked in her fiction often enough, practitioners of "that old-time religion" tend to speak the truth, even if they do so by accident.

This stumbling into the truth is what O'Connor meant by the term "wise blood." In the absence of sacraments, O'Connor believed, Protestants have to trust their instincts. It is a sloppy way of getting to the truth, but, she suggested, it sometimes works.

ɔʃɔ

Even as Flannery O'Connor was diligently cultivating her interest in popular culture, popular culture was cultivating an interest in her. Harvey Breit, assistant editor of the *New York Times Sunday Book Review*, invited her to be interviewed on his new books-and-authors show, *Galley Proof*, on May 31, 1955. In addition to the interview, three actors dramatized a scene from "The Life You Save May Be Your Own." "Do you reckon this is going to corrupt me?" she jokingly asked Robie Macauley. "I already feel like a combination of Msgr. Sheen [a Catholic radio and television celebrity] and Gorgeous George [a professional wrestler]."[16]

Galley Proof aired at 2:30 on Tuesday afternoon. O'Connor expressed some concern that children "waiting impatiently for *The Batman*" after school would be subjected to her "glacial glare" instead.[17] She didn't come across as especially comfortable in the interview; her answers to Breit's questions tended to be short, even curt. Breit was interested in her Southernness and asked a number of questions about regional influence in her writing. "What about those fascinating characters?" he asked. "Do you know them at all? Have you seen people like that?"

"Well, no, not really," O'Connor answered. "I've seen many people like that, I think, and I have seen myself. I think, putting all that together, you get these people." O'Connor insisted, however, that her stories are not "about" the South even though they are Southern: "A serious novelist is in pursuit of reality. And of course when you're a Southerner and in pursuit of reality, the reality you come up with is going to have a Southern accent, but that's just an accent; it's not the essence of what you're trying to do."

∞

After the partial dramatization of "The Life You Save May Be Your Own," Breit asked, "Flannery, would you like to tell our audience what happens in that story?" O'Connor was adamant: "No, I certainly would not. I don't think you can paraphrase a story like that. I think there's only one way to tell it and that's the way it is told in the story."[18]

She described her television experience as "mildly ghastly." She conducted other media interviews while in New York, but her heart wasn't in it. "I had interviews with this one and that one, ate with this one and that one . . . and generally managed to conduct myself as if this were all very well but I had business at home."[19]

Less than a week out from the publication of *A Good Man Is Hard to Find*, she found that the atmosphere at her publisher had "changed to one of eager enthusiasm." She noticed that her story collection was getting more attention than her novel had, and she hoped it would result in more sales. While she was in New York, she also signed a contract for the novel on which she had been working intermittently since shortly after *Wise Blood* was published.

There was another matter of business for O'Connor to tend to while she was in New York. At the end of March, Giroux had resigned from Harcourt to join Farrar, Straus, and Cudahy. O'Connor's new editor was Catharine Carver. This suited her fine; as she told Carver, "[Giroux] told me once that you did all the work anyhow, which was what I might have suspected."[20] She would come to trust Carver's literary judgment almost as much as she trusted Caroline Gordon's. But she wanted to be protected from any more changes to the editorial personnel. Katherine McKee, her agent, added a clause to her contract whereby she would be released from her contractual commitment to Harcourt should there be another change in editors.

𝒥𝒫

A Good Man Is Hard to Find and Other Stories was released on June 6, 1955. O'Connor dedicated the book to the Fitzgeralds ("Nine stories about original sin, with my compliments," she quipped when she told her friends about the honor[21]). She was correct in her guess that the extra attention to the book would translate into sales. Four thousand copies had sold by September—not blockbuster numbers, but better than respectable for a collection of short stories. In July, editor Catharine Carver reported that *A Good Man Is Hard to Find* was selling better than anything on their list except for the works of the Trappist monk Thomas Merton—"which doesn't say much for their list," O'Connor remarked.

As before, reviews for O'Connor's book were mixed. Caroline Gordon gave her friend a glowing review in the pages of the *New York Times Book Review*. "Miss O'Connor is as realistic and down to earth a writer as one can find," she wrote. "Yet many people profess to find her work hard to understand. This may be because she uses symbolism in a way in which it has not been used by any of her young contemporaries."[22]

Gordon's observation was borne out in the other reviews of *A Good Man Is Hard to Find*, both positive and negative. *Time* referred to the stories as "witheringly sarcastic," marred by "arty fumbling" whenever she left aside brutal directness and groped for deeper meaning. The *Time* review again drew parallels between her work and that of Erskine Caldwell: "The South that simpers, storms and snivels in these pages moves along a sort of up-to-date Tobacco Road, paved right into town."[23] O'Connor wrote that this particular review "nearly gave me apoplexy."[24]

The *Kenyon Review*, which had first published several of the stories included in *A Good Man Is Hard to Find*, ran a review that described the book as "profane, blasphemous, and outrageous," though the reviewer didn't seem to think that was necessarily a bad thing. "Miss O'Connor is consistent in her condemnation," the reviewer wrote. "Her tremendous catalogue of her society's ills is like a medical lexicon of symptoms looking for a body."[25]

The notice in the *Kenyon Review* wasn't, in fact, a negative review. But, in O'Connor's mind, it was one of many that utterly missed the point of what she was trying to do in her stories. "I am mighty tired of reading reviews that call *A Good Man* brutal and sarcastic," she wrote.

> The stories are hard but they are hard because there is nothing harder or less sentimental than Christian realism. I believe that there are many rough beasts now slouching toward Bethlehem to be born and that I have reported the progress of a few of them, and when I see these stories described as horror stories I am always amused because the reviewer always has hold of the wrong horror.[26]

For O'Connor, the real horror was never violence or deformity, but damnation. Horror that awakens a soul to its own danger and prepares it to receive grace is no horror, but a mercy.

"The devil," she wrote, "accomplishes a good deal of groundwork that seems to be necessary before grace is effective."[27]

O'Connor's reception among fellow Catholics was scarcely better than her reception by the critics. After publishing "A Temple of the Holy Ghost," she received a letter from a woman in Boston. "She said she was a Catholic and so she couldn't understand how anybody could even HAVE such thoughts." O'Connor won the woman over with a letter so orthodox in its theology that it "could have been signed by the bishop."[28]

From Graham Greene and Evelyn Waugh to Caroline Gordon and Walker Percy, there were a number of Catholic writers who were committed to the highest literary standards in the middle of the twentieth century. But much of what passed for "Catholic literature" was written in what O'Connor called the pious style. Remarking on the work of another Catholic writer, she commented that it "is just propaganda and its being propaganda for the side of the angels only makes it worse. The novel is an art form and when you use it for anything other than art, you pervert it."[29]

In "The Church and the Fiction Writer," an essay in the Catholic journal *America* that began as a lecture at a Macon women's club, O'Connor addresses the false literary notions of many of her co-religionists: "It is generally supposed, and not least by Catholics, that the Catholic who writes fiction is out to use fiction to prove the truth of the Faith, or at the least, to prove the existence of the supernatural." But if it is apparent in the finished work that "pertinent actions have been fraudulently manipulated or overlooked or smothered" for the purposes of pushing through any agenda, the work fails artistically—and fails to push through its agenda as well. Even the well-intentioned writer "cannot move or mold reality in the interests of abstract truth."[30]

The duty of the fiction writer—the Christian writer no less than any other writer—is to look clearly and fearlessly at what is—not what ought to be—and to use those concrete facts as the raw material for fiction. Ironically, it is only when the fiction writer obeys the laws of his or her art, rather than resorting to propaganda, that the sense of the Transcendent has a chance to exert itself. "When fiction is made according to its nature, it should reinforce our sense of the supernatural by grounding it in concrete, observable reality."[31]

O'Connor also argued, "If the Catholic writer hopes to reveal mysteries, he will have to do it by describing truthfully what he sees from where he is. An affirmative vision cannot be demanded of him without limiting his freedom to observe what man has done with the things of God." O'Connor was happy to leave trite affirmation to the Dr. Cranes of the world. Her work was to reveal mysteries, and that required the freedom to range over the whole world of "what is," even in all its ugliness.

9 | "THE ACCURATE NAMING OF THE THINGS OF GOD": 1955–1956

In July 1955, O'Connor received a fan letter that interested her very much. It came from a young woman named Elizabeth Hester, a credit company clerk in Atlanta, who obviously understood that O'Connor was trying to accomplish something immensely important in her "God-conscious" fiction. She wrote back to Hester, "I am very pleased to have your letter. Perhaps it is even more startling to me to find someone who recognizes my work for what I try to make it than it is for you to find a God-conscious writer near at hand. The distance is 87 miles but I feel the spiritual distance is shorter."[1]

This was the first of 150 letters that O'Connor would write to Betty Hester over the remaining nine years of her life. In the body of O'Connor's letters, these are unique in their openness. In her letters to Hester, O'Connor revealed her inner workings in ways she rarely did in her other letters. She spoke of her father and of the true nature of her illness—topics that she almost never committed to writing.

In *The Habit of Being*, Sally Fitzgerald concealed Hester's identity, calling her "A" at Hester's request. A private person, Betty asked that she not be identified until after her death, which came by suicide on Christmas Day 1998. The eagerness with which O'Connor pursued this epistolary relationship suggests how lonely she was for intellectually stimulating conversation. Though the trip from Atlanta to Milledgeville was an easy one (Hester was acquainted with O'Connor's uncle Louis Cline in Atlanta and could have caught a ride any time she wanted), O'Connor and Hester met in person only a few times. As Sally Fitzgerald points out in a note in *The Habit of Being*, "We are fortunate that they met late, and not very frequently, so that all she had to say to this almost uniquely important friend did not go up in talk but had to be written down."[2]

Besides being intelligent, well-read, and intellectually curious, Betty Hester was also an agnostic with a genuine interest in knowing more about God and the Church. This was unmistakably a genuine friendship and not a burden for O'Connor. ("I have no letter-writing duties," she wrote to Hester. "Anyway, be it understood that my writing to you is a free act, unconnected with character, duty or compulsion."[3]) Nevertheless, O'Connor's letters do from time to time give the impression that she viewed her agnostic friend as a personal project. She took it upon herself to articulate what she believed in terms that would make as much sense as possible to a person who does not share her beliefs.

The story of Flannery O'Connor's life is the story of her inner life more than her outer life. The Betty Hester letters, like nothing else in the body of O'Connor's work, shed light on that inner life—who she was as a believer, as a writer, as a Southerner, as a human being. There is still plenty of wit and polish in these letters, but there is something more immediate in the way she reveals herself.

In her first letter to Hester, O'Connor wrote,

I write the way I do because (not though) I am a Catholic. This is a fact and nothing covers it like the bald statement. However, I am a Catholic peculiarly possessed of the modern consciousness, that thing Jung describes as unhistorical, solitary, and guilty. To possess this within the church is to bear a burden, the necessary burden for the conscious Catholic. It's to feel the contemporary situation at the ultimate level. I think that the Church is the only thing that is going to make the terrible world we are coming to endurable; the only thing that makes the Church endurable is that it is somehow the body of Christ and that on this we are fed. It seems to be a fact that you have to suffer as much from the Church as for it but if you believe in the divinity of Christ, you have to cherish the world at the same time that you struggle to endure it. This may explain the lack of bitterness in the stories.[4]

That idea of the interaction between ultimate truth on the one hand and a modern, skeptical, and self-sufficient unbelief on the other is a key to O'Connor's vision of her project. In her next letter to Hester she wrote, "My audience are the people who think God is dead. At least these are the people I am conscious of writing for."[5] And writing for such people required that she find a whole new language. A writer like Dante, living in the thirteenth century, had the luxury of sharing a basic set of convictions with his readership. By contrast, O'Connor had to make up a new literary means of communication for her natively unsympathetic audience, drawing startling and large figures to get the attention of the almost blind, shouting in the ear of the almost deaf.

O'Connor's grand theological pronouncements were balanced, however, by quieter remarks in which she revealed to Hester her own doubts and shortcomings. "My virtues are as timid as my vices," she confessed. "I think sin occasionally brings one closer to God, but not habitual sin and not this petty kind that blocks every small good."[6] In only her second letter to Hester, O'Connor confessed her own struggles to believe:

> When I ask myself how I know I believe, I have no satisfactory answer at all, no assurance at all, no feeling at all. I can only say with Peter, Lord I believe, help my unbelief. And all I can say about my love of God, is, Lord help me in my lack of it. I distrust pious phrases, particularly when they issue from my mouth. [7]

O'Connor's letters to Hester come back again and again to the question of what one is supposed to *feel* about the truths of the faith. Hester, it seems, was looking for some sort of emotional satisfaction before she was willing to submit to the claims of Christ. O'Connor insisted that she was not especially interested in how Hester or anybody else feels about the faith. "I can never agree with you that the Incarnation, or any truth, has to satisfy emotionally to be right . . . there are long periods in the lives of all of us, and of the saints, when the truth as revealed by faith is hideous, emotionally disturbing, downright repulsive."[8]

O'Connor's language rarely seemed calculated to make a convert of Hester. Rather, she was content to tell the truth as she perceived it and leave the rest in other hands than hers.

One thing that rings clear in O'Connor's correspondence with Hester, and elsewhere, is the thoroughness with which she integrated her theological vision with her vision of her work as a writer. The moral basis of fiction and poetry, she wrote to Hester, "is the accurate naming of the things of God." Clarifying the phrase in a later letter, she said, "It's only trying to see straight and it's the least you can set yourself to do, the least you can ask for. You ask God to let you see straight and write straight."[9]

Seeing straight, for O'Connor, first meant seeing *this* world and from here learning to see another world. "For me the visible universe is a reflection of the invisible universe," she wrote.[10] The visible universe is one way eternal truths are bodied forth. Another is through story—the accurate naming of the things of God. And the most important was the sacraments.

O'Connor could be touchy on this point; she was unwilling to allow anyone to reduce the sacraments to mere symbols. She described a dinner party at which she was discussing the Eucharist with author Mary McCarty and her husband, Bowden Broadwater. McCarty said that she regarded the Eucharist as a symbol, and a good one. O'Connor, who by her account had been quiet most of the night, finally spoke up in a shaky voice: "'Well, if it's a symbol, to hell with it.' That was all the defense I was capable of but I realize not that this is all I will ever be able to say about it, outside of a story, except that it is the center of existence for me; all the rest of life is expendable."[11]

That's one of the most well-known anecdotes in all of O'Connor lore, largely because it is so typically O'Connor: the shocking statement in the service of the oldest kind of orthodoxy. Unorthodox orthodoxy. As shocking as the grotesqueries in her fiction are, none is so shocking as the realization that they are marshaled in the service of a Catholic orthodoxy that the author submits to—or, in any case, wishes to submit to—without the least trace of ironic detachment.

A young writer once asked O'Connor to look over an article that she was writing for *Mademoiselle* magazine on the subject of O'Connor's work. Speaking of "A Good Man Is Hard to Find," the young woman wrote, "[O'Connor] merely states that it is probably impossible to know how to be one [a good man]." O'Connor took exception to that assessment. "Not at all," she said. "It is possible to know how to be one. God became man partly in order to teach us, but it is impossible to be one without the help of grace." It was an answer worthy of the most conventional Sunday school teacher out there. To the disappointed young writer O'Connor continued,

> The truth in any such matter is always a great deal more stodgy-sounding than what we would like to believe. Many of my ardent admirers would be roundly shocked and disturbed if they realized that everything I believe is thoroughly moral, thoroughly Catholic, and that it is these beliefs that give my work its chief characteristics. [12]

✧

In August 1955, O'Connor stopped taking ACTH injections to control her lupus and started taking prednisone pills, "the newest wonder drug." For the first time in four years she would neither have to give herself shots nor tightly control her salt intake.

But the good news on the lupus front was partially neutralized by bad news on the rheumatism front. X-rays revealed that the top of her leg bone was softening as the result of poor circulation in the hip. "I got this *straight*," she emphasized to Sally

Fitzgerald, "having seen the X rays and spoken with the scientist *before* the parental conference."[13] No longer would she get her medical information as filtered through her mother.

Dr. Merrill ordered a couple of years on crutches in hopes that keeping weight off the hip would give it a chance to harden again. Otherwise she could be faced with surgery or a wheelchair. "What's two or three years off your life?" he asked rhetorically, having no way of knowing that his patient had less than eight years to live. The doctor assured O'Connor again that her hip trouble was not directly related to the lupus. Later research has revealed, however, that joint trouble like O'Connor's could be a side effect of the high doses of corticosteroids that she had taken for four years.[14]

O'Connor was characteristically flippant about this latest setback, making it the stuff of anecdote in her letters. In the elevator of the Davison's department store in Atlanta, a solicitous old woman stared and said, "Bless you, darling!" O'Connor did not take it well: "I felt exactly like the Misfit and gave her a weakly lethal look, whereupon greatly encouraged, she grabbed my arm and whispered (very loud) in my ear, 'Remember what they said to John at the gate, Darling!'" O'Connor escaped the next time the elevator opened, "and I suppose the old lady was astounded at how quick I could get away on crutches." A one-legged friend told O'Connor that the old woman in speaking of John at the gate, must have been referring to the phrase "The lame shall enter first," which would soon be the title of an O'Connor story. "This may be because the lame will be able to knock everybody aside with their crutches," O'Connor suggested.[15]

After the publication of *A Good Man Is Hard to Find*, O'Connor took a break from writing short stories and picked up her novel again. In the fall of 1955, the first chapter would be published in *New World Writing* as a story called "You Can't Be Any Poorer than Dead." She continued to make slow progress.

In December, O'Connor was distressed to learn that Catharine Carver would be leaving Harcourt. Technically, Carver's departure voided her contract for the novel. But she liked and trusted Denver Lindley, the editor who would be picking up where Carver left off, so she stayed wit Harcourt. She had the contract amended again, inserting Lindley's name in the clause where Carver's name had been. Even though Carver went to Viking, O'Connor would continue to send manuscripts to her for comments, just as she did with Caroline Gordon.

"I am never prepared for anything," O'Connor wrote to Betty Hester in January 1956. She had just learned that Hester had converted to Catholicism.

> I have been equally positive . . . that you were a Pantheist in good standing . . . and now you allow you're as orthodox as I am if not more. More, I suppose, as baptism is something you choose and I had it thrust upon me. To my credit it can be said anyway that I never considered you unbaptized. There are the three kinds, of water, blood, and desire, and with the last I thought you as baptized as I am. . . . All voluntary baptisms are a miracle to me and stop my mouth as much as if I had just seen Lazarus walk out of the tomb.[16]

When Hester was confirmed in the church a few months later, O'Connor was her proud sponsor. It seems that when

Hester asked O'Connor to be her sponsor, she felt the need to share some details about her own "horrible history." Perhaps her recent conversion had put her in a confessional mood, or perhaps she felt sullied and wanted to give O'Connor a chance to distance herself if she were so inclined. It is not clear how much Hester told of her story, but it was indeed a horrible one. Her father abandoned the family when Betty was young; at the age of thirteen, she watched her mother commit suicide. There was more, but it is almost certain that she didn't tell it at that time. It is possible that she didn't tell any of it at that time, but was only offering to tell. In any case, O'Connor reassured her. "As for your horrible history, that has nothing to do with it. I'm interested in the history because it's you but not for this or any other occasion."[17]

The spring of 1956 brought a trip to Lansing, Michigan, where O'Connor addressed the American Association of University Women on the subject of "The Significance of the Short Story." She told Robie Macauley, "I don't have the foggiest notion what the significance of the short story is but I accepted at once as I like to make trips by plane, etc., and I figured I had ten months to find out. . . . Maybe I'll write Dr. Crane and ask him what the significance of the short story is. He tackles *any* subject."[18] O'Connor survived the talk and the National Association of Catholic Women luncheon that was tacked onto it. ("If ever there has been designed something suitable for the remission of temporal punishment due to sin, this is it," she joked to Hester.[19]) She also made another round of Middle Georgia ladies' clubs that spring and summer.

It was that spring that O'Connor learned that she would not be on crutches for only a year or two or three. "It's crutches for me from here on out," she reported to Hester. An X-ray revealed that the bone was too diseased either to heal itself or to be capped surgically. "So, so much for that," she said dismissively. "I will henceforth be a structure with flying buttresses."[20]

The summer brought the publication of "Greenleaf," which featured yet another widow in charge of a farm. Mrs. May, who meets her end when she is gored by a bull, so closely resembles Regina O'Connor that Flannery's friend Maryat Lee said she had gotten away with murder.[21] The story won the O. Henry Award that year, O'Connor's second.

The summer also brought Betty Hester, in the flesh, to Andalusia. It was not an altogether comfortable meeting. Hester was quite reclusive, and she seemed uneasy in the presence of the woman she was so comfortable with in her letters. After the visit O'Connor wrote, "I had the impression that all the time you were here you were poised for flight—a lark with a jet engine—and that if I turned my back, you would have been gone."[22] For O'Connor, at least, that first meeting seems to have been overshadowed by the gap between the way she imagined Hester from her letters and the way she perceived her in person. Apparently Hester's description of her own appearance was too humble by half. O'Connor wrote, "You don't look anything like I expected you to as I always take people at their word and I was prepared for white hair, horn-rimmed spectacles, nose of eagle and shape of ginger-beer bottle. Seek the truth and pursue it; you ain't even passably ugly." The two women settled right back into their more comfortable epistolary friendship.

The summer of 1956 was also the summer of the telephone at Andalusia. "A great invention," O'Connor judged. "A great mother-saver."[23] Bigger news than the new telephone, however, was the new refrigerator—"the kind that spits the ice cubes at you, the trays shoot out and hit you in the stomach, and if you step on a certain button, the whole thing glides from the wall and knocks you down."[24] The new refrigerator was purchased with the funds from the sale of the television rights for "The Life You Save Might Be Your Own."

In 1953, Georgia Power had begun filling Lake Sinclair, a fifteen-thousand-acre reservoir outside of Milledgeville. Farms and pastures, forests and homeplaces were bought and sold and submerged. Farmland became suddenly valuable lakefront property. Parts of the new lake were as close as three miles from Andalusia. Lake Sinclair was apparently on O'Connor's mind in the fall of 1956 as she wrote "A View of the Woods," a story with the kind of complex family drama one would expect in a Greek tragedy. A grandfather, blinded by greed and hubris, kills his granddaughter, the one person he loves, while a great yellow bulldozer churns up the family farm to make a place for the obliterating waters of a new lake. As she did so often, O'Connor turned her immediate locale into a setting almost as mythic as Oedipus's Thebes or Medea's Colchis. Middle Georgia was O'Connor's Ithaka, her Troy. After being rejected by *Harper's*, "A View of the Woods" was accepted by *Partisan Review* and would be published a year later, in the fall 1957 issue.

In October 1956 Betty Hester, who had told (or at least tried to tell) O'Connor part of her life story in the previous spring, wrote a letter detailing her darkest secret. As a younger woman, she had been dishonorably discharged from the military for a sexual indiscretion, probably with another woman. Her famous friend, she realized, could suffer harm as the result of associating with a person who had a lesbian scandal in her past.

O'Connor's letter in reply is a beautiful expression of loyalty and grace:

> I can't write you fast enough and tell you that it doesn't make the slightest bit of difference in my opinion of you, which is the same as it was, and that is based solidly on complete respect. . . . Compared to what you have experienced in the way of radical misery, I have never had anything to bear in my life but minor irritations. But there are times when the sharpest suffering is not to suffer and the worst affliction not to be afflicted. Job's comforters were worse off than he was, though they didn't know it. If in any sense my knowing your burden can make your burden lighter, then I am doubly glad I know it. You are right to tell me. But I'm glad you didn't tell me until I knew you well. Where you are wrong is in saying that you *are* a history of horror. The meaning of the Redemption is precisely that we do not have to *be* our history, and nothing is plainer to me than that you are not your history. [25]

Meanwhile, news—delightfully tacky news—about the television play of "The Life You Save" began trickling into Milledgeville, reported by friends who read the gossip columns in the New York papers. At first O'Connor thought the play was going to be presented by the General Electric Playhouse, but then it turned out the not-quite-as-respectable-sounding Schlitz Playhouse would be presenting it. For a while O'Connor thought Mr. Shiftlet might be played by Ronald Reagan, but then she found out that the lead would be "a tap-dancer by the name of Gene Kelly," who described the story as "a kind of hillbilly thing in which I play a guy who *befriends* [emphasis O'Connor's] a deaf-mute girl in the hills of Kentucky. It gives me a great chance to do some straight acting, something I really have no opportunity to do in movies."[26] Whatever the details, however, O'Connor was confident that the television people would butcher her story. "Mr. Shiftlet and the idiot daughter will no doubt go off in a Chrysler and live happily ever after. Anyway . . . while they make hash out of my story, [Regina] and me will make ice in the new refrigerator."[27]

The show aired on March 1, 1957. The O'Connors did not have a television, so they went to Aunt Mary Cline's house to watch with the college librarian and several "old local ladies." O'Connor reported that she was "not overcome by [Gene Kelly's] acting powers. . . . The best I can say for it is that conceivably it could have been worse. Just conceivably."[28] But the play itself wasn't nearly as hard to swallow as the reaction of the townspeople. "They feel that I have arrived at last," she complained. "They are willing to forget that the original story was not as good as the television play. Children now point to me on the street. It's mighty disheartening."[29]

When she heard a rumor (surely tongue-in-cheek) that somebody had contacted Rodgers and Hammerstein about a musical adaptation of "The Life You Save May Be Your Own," O'Connor contributed some lyrics:

> The life you save may be your own
> Hand me that there tellyphone
> Hideho and hip hooray
> I am in this thang for pay.[30]

10 | "THE SOCIETY I FEED ON": 1957–1958

In December 1956, a most unlikely friend entered Flannery O'Connor's life. Maryat Lee was the sister of Dr. Robert E. Lee, the newly appointed president of Georgia State College for Women. A flamboyant, opinionated, unorthodox playwright, she came down to Milledgeville from New York City to spend the holidays with her brother and her family.

Lee was unfamiliar with O'Connor's work. When O'Connor called on the last day of Lee's visit and invited her to come out to Andalusia, Lee came with reluctance, afraid that she would be stuck spending the last day of her vacation in the presence of a Southern "lady writer." But she went anyway, and they hit it off immediately. In many ways, the two women were polar opposites. Lee lived a bohemian lifestyle in New York; O'Connor lived on the farm with her mother. Lee's politics were liberal and activist; O'Connor's were conservative and laissez-faire. Lee, though born in Kentucky, was a naturalized Northerner and urbanite; O'Connor was a small town Southerner.

Nevertheless, Maryat Lee and Flannery O'Connor liked each other very much and became frequent correspondents. The letters they exchanged are easily the funniest and most outlandish in O'Connor's correspondence. Exaggerating their differences, Lee and O'Connor had a running odd-couple act—O'Connor's redneck realist to Lee's effete idealist. The South and race relations were common topics in their correspondence; O'Connor's devil's advocacy of reactionary segregationism against Lee's progressive, integrationist politics is usually played for laughs, but it can get ugly nevertheless. O'Connor's views on race are complex and sometimes self-contradictory. Her letters to Lee are a rich source for understanding where she stood.

Lee's first visit to Milledgeville ended with a minor scandal—or, rather, potential scandal—that set the tone for the women's ongoing correspondence. When it came time for Lee to return to the Atlanta airport, she got a ride from her brother's gardener, a black man named Emmett. Regina O'Connor was mortified. "Don't you tell a soul that she is going in Emmett's car," she warned Flannery. "Don't you even tell Sister [Aunt Mary Cline]. If that got out, it would ruin Dr. Lee."

Dr. Lee, however, took steps to keep it from getting out. When he saw Mary, he lied and told her that Maryat had caught a ride to Atlanta with friends. "I think Dr. Lee will last a long time here," O'Connor wrote; "in fact as long as he cares to last."[1]

"It is so funny that you forget it is also terrible," she wrote—a perfectly Flannery formulation. She recalled a teachers' conference ten years earlier that was attended by two black educators. The president of the college had gone to the trouble to install "separate and equal" everything, including Coca-Cola machines, to prevent any mixing of the races. But still a cross was burned in his yard. "The people who burned the cross couldn't have gone past the fourth grade but, for the time, they were mighty inter-ested in education."[2]

A taste for the ridiculous, which she shared with Lee, shaped the way O'Connor wrote to her friend about race. She spoke of a recent cross "burning" in which the Klan, instead of torching a wooden cross, plugged in a portable one that was illuminated with red electric bulbs: "When I saw that, I said to myself: this is mighty disheartening, it is later than I think."[3]

But if O'Connor thought the local rednecks ridiculous, she thought outside agitators who came south to help fight for civil rights just as ridiculous. Dorothy Day, the Catholic social activ-ist, came to Koinonia, an interracial agricultural cooperative in South Georgia. While standing watch one night, Day was shot at; the bullets narrowly missed her. O'Connor usually admired Day, but she couldn't muster much sympathy this time. She wrote to Lee, "All my thoughts on this subject are ugly and unchari-table—such as: that's a mighty long way to come to get shot at, etc. I admire her very much. I still think of the story about the Tennessee hillbilly who picked up his gun and said, 'I'm going to Texas to fight fuhmuh rights.' I hope that to be of two minds about some things is not to be neutral."[4]

When Maryat Lee asked O'Connor how she would feel about the black author James Baldwin coming to visit her, O'Connor was adamant:

No I can't see James Baldwin in Georgia. It would cause the greatest trouble and disturbance and disunion. In New York it would be nice to meet him; here it would not. I observe the traditions of the society I feed on—it's only fair. Might as well expect a mule to fly as me to see James Baldwin in Georgia. I have read one of his stories and it was a good one.[5]

The troubling thing about O'Connor, perhaps, is not the fact that she had two minds about racial issues, but that she seemed to enter so easily and comfortably into the mind of the bigot. She could be free with the word *nigger* and she loved to tell stories that portrayed the black people in her life as hapless children. In her unpublished letters to Maryat Lee, she freely shared racist jokes that she had picked up around Milledgeville.

In fairness to O'Connor, the self that she portrayed in the Maryat Lee letters was a caricature. She was ventriloquizing, playing a part as surely as if she were an actress on a stage. Indeed, as Ralph C. Wood points out, the use of private correspondence to make judgments or draw conclusions about what a person "really" thinks is a tricky business. What looks like candor may actually be "superficial opinions that have been tossed off in a trice and thus never meant for conclusion-drawing scrutiny."[6] Wood also points out that none of O'Connor's contemporaries—not even Maryat Lee—ever accused her of racism. And in O'Connor's stories, black characters come off as looking better than their white counterparts in almost every way.

The discomfort a twenty-first-century reader feels with O'Connor's use of racial slurs or even racial jokes is not the most relevant fact in an examination of O'Connor's racist positions. More relevant, perhaps, is the fact that she expressed indignation toward Northern liberals who came south to get mixed up in racial politics, and yet she never demonstrated much indignation at the violent injustices that were visited on Southern blacks. O'Connor's commitment to gradual, organic change looks suspiciously like the path of least resistance for her time and place. When it came to racial attitudes, O'Connor was at the progressive end of the normal range for Southerners of the 1950s and early '60s. But she was still in the normal range.

In *Flannery O'Connor and the Christ-Haunted South*, Ralph Wood offers as much insight as anybody into Flannery O'Connor's racial attitudes and what they mean. He does not quite defend her from charges of racism. Instead, he makes a convincing case that her willingness to acknowledge her own incipient racism—indeed, her "self-mocking tone" on the subject—"was her prophylactic against any easy contempt for the unenlightened, any easy self-congratulation for her own kind." By Wood's logic, the easy rectitude of racial liberalism invites a self-righteousness that is even more dangerous to the soul than racism. Wood invokes Neibuhr: "The Christian doctrine of the sinfulness of all men is thus a constant challenge to re-examine superficial moral judgments, particularly those which self-righteously give the moral advantage to the one who makes the judgment."[7]

To say that Flannery O'Connor was a product of her time is not to let her off the hook when it comes to matters of race. She could have been much more progressive than she was without any real danger of losing herself in self-righteousness. But she did possess an unusual amount of self-awareness; she understood that her own soul trouble—all of our soul trouble—runs much deeper than racism.

℘

For a Southern writer, any discussion of race goes hand-in-hand, of course, with a discussion of region. O'Connor's commitment to the South as "the society I feed on" grew stronger the longer she lived there. When she received a letter from Maryat Lee suggesting that Lee might be moving back to the South, O'Connor exclaimed,

So it may be the South! You get no condolences from me. This is a Return I have faced and when I faced it I was roped and tied and resigned the way it is necessary to be resigned to death, and largely because I thought it would be the end of any creation, any writing, any work from me. And . . . it was only the beginning.[8]

O'Connor expressed irritation at non-Southerners like Wallace Stegner who were advising Southern writers to leave the South and forget the myth. "Which myth?" she asked. "If you're a writer and the South is what you know, then it's what you'll write about and how you'll judge yourself." For O'Connor, it had very little to do with romanticizing or mythologizing the South and much more with a matter-of-fact realization that one's native land, in a practical sense, provides the raw materials for writing.

This is not to say that what the South gives is enough, or that it is even significant in any but a practical way—as in providing the texture and the idiom and so forth. But these things have to be provided. . . . The advantages and disadvantages of being a Southern writer can be endlessly debated but the fact remains that if you are, you are.[9]

In any case, she noted, she had done her best writing since returning to Georgia. In one regard, however, O'Connor did make special claims for the South as a wellspring of literary culture. In the "Christ-haunted" South, she argued, the doctrines of sin and grace and redemption still held sway. Elsewhere, where a secular approach prevails, the writer is forced to make bricks without the benefit of straw: "The Liberal approach is that man has never fallen, never incurred guilt, and is ultimately perfectible by his own efforts. Therefore, evil in this light is a problem of better housing, sanitation, health, etc. and all mysteries will eventually be cleared up."[10]

All of which helps to explain why Southern literature, in O'Connor's view, is so often misunderstood outside the region. O'Connor observed, "I have found that anything that comes out of the South is going to be called grotesque by the Northern reader, unless it is grotesque, in which case it is going to be called realistic."[11] And if Southern writers have a tendency to write about freaks, O'Connor remarked, "it is because we are still able to recognize one."[12]

જ્ઞ

In 1957 O'Connor again laid aside short-story writing to focus on the novel that she had been under contract to write since 1955. It was a tough slog. That summer she finally began gravitating toward the phrase that would be the title of the book: *The Violent Bear It Away*. It comes from Matthew 11:12, the Douay-Rheims translation: "And from the days of John the Baptist until now, the kingdom of heaven suffereth violence, and the violent bear it away." It is an apt image for O'Connor's entire body of work: "And more than ever now it seems that the kingdom of heaven has to be taken by violence, or not at all. You have to push as hard as the age that pushes against you."[13] That push, that willingness to offend, that violence and extremity, these are the essence of O'Connor's prophetic instinct.

In late July, O'Connor got an encouraging X-ray. The bone in her hip appeared to be mending; Dr. Merrill told O'Connor she could expect to be off her crutches in two to three years. "So that is fine," she said. "I want to stomp around when I get to be an old lady."[14]

Cousin Katie had another idea for getting Flannery on her feet: a seventeen-day pilgrimage to Europe, particularly Rome and Lourdes, France. In the extreme south of France, almost in Spain, Lourdes was the site where, in 1858, a peasant girl named Bernadette Soubirous reported seeing an apparition of the Virgin Mary on eighteen different occasions. The water from the grotto at Lourdes reportedly had healing properties; from the mid-nineteenth century to today, the sick and lame and other pilgrims have come by the millions to visit the chapel built on the site, and to drink and bathe in the waters. It was Cousin Katie's notion to get Flannery to the waters at Lourdes and pray for a miraculous healing.

At Lourdes, the sanctuary grounds themselves are beautiful, but just outside the gates is a strip of religious souvenir shops as tacky and commercialized as anything found in an American tourist trap. The combination of maimed pilgrims and vulgarized religion, was O'Connor's metier. She told Betty Hester, "I am all for it too though I expect it to be a comic nightmare."[15] The trip was scheduled for April and May 1958.

Meanwhile, O'Connor spent December writing "The Enduring Chill," a story in which a young writer named Asbury comes home from New York City to his small Southern town, fully prepared to die of what he believes to be a lethal disease. Unlike his creator, however, Asbury discovers that his disease is not fatal after all. In the end, his tragedy turns out to be not that he is dying, but that he will continue to live with his insufferable self under the same roof with a mother and sister he cannot abide.

That winter O'Connor also joined a book club put together by an Episcopal minister to talk about theology in modern literature. The attendees were mostly Presbyterians and Episcopalians ("and me as the representative of the Holy Roman Catholic &

Apostolic Church"[16]). But she found herself in a bit of a quandary. The book list included the French writer André Gide. And Gide was on the *Index Librorum Prohibitorum*—the list of prohibited by Catholic authorities. A good Catholic was not to read a book that was on the *Index* without first getting express permission from church officials.

It would have been easy enough, of course, to ignore the prohibition. There were no other Catholics in her reading group, and the Protestants who selected Gide probably didn't know he was on the *Index*; or if they knew they didn't care.

Nevertheless, the thirty-two-year-old O'Connor wrote to her Jesuit friend Father J. H. McCown to see if he would be able to grant her the necessary permission to read the book. It was a moment of remarkable humility. Father McCown was an intelligent and well-read man. But still, for O'Connor to seek his permission in this matter was to submit her superb literary judgment to another kind of judgment altogether.

In seeking Father McCown's permission to read a book on the *Index*, O'Connor was submitting her formidable intellect to an authority capable of restraining its sinful yearnnig for autonomy, as she explained to newly converted Betty Hester:

> I doubt if your interests get less intellectual as you become more deeply involved in the Church, but what will happen is that the intellect will take its place in a larger context and will cease to be tyrannical, if it has been—and when there is nothing over the intellect it usually is tyrannical.[17]

The trip to Lourdes, in its way, was another blow against the tyranny of the intellect for O'Connor. She scorned all miracle-mongering Catholicism, and she had no intention of bathing at

Lourdes. "I am one of those people who could die for his religion easier than take a bath for it," she wrote to Hester. "If there were any danger of my having to take one, I would not go. I don't think I'd mind washing in somebody else's blood . . . but the lack of privacy would be what I couldn't stand. This is neither right nor holy of me but it is what is."[18]

O'Connor went to Lourdes in large part because she was bullied into it. At first Dr. Merrill refused to give her permission to travel overseas. But Cousin Katie insisted, working up a plan whereby Flannery and Regina would skip most of the tour of Ireland and France, joining the group at Lourdes and continuing on to Rome. As O'Connor told Betty Hester, "It is Cousin Katie's end-all and be-all that I get to Lourdes and if I am dead upon arrival that's too bad but I still have to get there."[19] O'Connor spun a fantasy of herself and her mother, alone in Europe, accidentally finding themselves behind the Iron Curtain and asking the way to Lourdes in sign language. "Cousin Katie has a will of iron," she complained. "My will is apparently made out of a feather duster."[20] Dr. Merrill's will, like O'Connor's, was bent to Cousin Katie's; he acceded to her traveling to Europe.

Flannery and Regina flew to Milan on April 24 and spent four days with the Fitzgeralds in the coastal town of Levanto. From there they joined Cousin Katie and the rest of the pilgrimage in Paris, bringing Sally Fitzgerald with them.

"Lourdes was not as bad as I expected it to be," O'Connor reported to Elizabeth Bishop. "Somebody in Paris told me the miracle at Lourdes is that there are no epidemics and I found this to be the truth. Apparently nobody catches anything. The water in the baths is changed once a day, regardless of how many people get into it."[21]

O'Connor did, in fact, get in the bath, at the urging of both her cousin and, perhaps more persuasively, Sally Fitzgerald, who told her that not to bathe "would have been a failure to cooperate with grace."[22] Even after the fact, O'Connor never described her decision as an act of faith, but as deriving from "a selection of bad motives, such as to prevent any bad conscience for not having done it, and because it seemed at the time that it must be what was wanted of me."[23] She also candidly confessed that she prayed more for her ailing novel (*The Violent Bear It Away*) than for her ailing body.

"Les malades" waiting to bathe passed around a Thermos bottle of Lourdes water to share its supposed healing properties. O'Connor had a cold at the time, "so I figured I left more germs than I took away," she told a friend. The "sack" she wore in the bath had been used by the previous malade, "regardless of what ailed him." The other supplicants at the bath were all peasants according to O'Connor's account, and she "was very conscious of the distinct odor of the crowd. The supernatural is a fact there but it displaces nothing natural; except maybe those germs."[24]

As for the town of Lourdes itself, O'Connor described it as "a beautiful little village pockmarked with religious junk shops. . . . Mauriac wrote somewhere that the religious-goods stores were the devil's answer there to the Virgin Mary. Anyway, it's apparent that the devil has a good deal to answer to."[25]

Rome was the last stop on the pilgrimage. The archbishop had arranged for O'Connor's group to be on the front row during the general audience at St. Peter's. After the service, Pope Pius XII came down to greet the pilgrims and, having been requested by the archbishop, gave O'Connor a special blessing on account of her illness. "There is a wonderful radiance and liveliness about the old man," O'Connor said of the pope. "He fairly springs up and down the little steps to his chair. Whatever the special super-aliveness that holiness is, it is very apparent in him."[26]

On returning to Georgia, O'Connor sent a stateside report to her friend Bill Sessions; her nose for the ridiculous and the macabre was as sharp as ever:

> All middle Georgia is agog over a Mrs. Lyles from Macon who has just been discovered to have lost her two husbands (successive) mother-in-law and daughter by putting ant poison in their food. It appears she has been a voodoo practicer for the last number of years but everyone in Macon thought she was "lovely." Well, back to normal.[27]

Being back in Georgia meant being back on the novel—not a prospect O'Connor relished. She wrote to Betty Hester, "From here on out my novel will have to be forced by will. There is no pleasure left in it for me. How I would like to be writing something I could enjoy."[28] Only a week later, however, she seemed to be feeling better about her book-in-progress. She wrote to Cecil Dawkins that her vacation from *The Violent Bear It Away* had helped. "I am at it with something like vigor."[29]

Her newfound vigor could have been related to a reunion with an old favorite editor, Robert Giroux. Denver Lindley left Harcourt in the spring of 1958. Having bumped from Robert Giroux to Catharine Carver to Lindley, O'Connor had nowhere else to go at Harcourt. She invoked the release provision of her contract and signed a new contract with Giroux, then at Farrar, Straus, and Cudahy, for the publication of *The Violent Bear It Away*. The firm would eventually become Farrar, Straus and Giroux.

Besides working on the novel, O'Connor spent part of her summer practicing for the driving test. She failed her first try. ("This was just to prove I ain't adjusted to the modern world."[30]) But on her second try she passed with a 77 and, at the age of thirty-three, received her first driver's license. With a new driver in the family, the O'Connors soon got a new car. Not surprisingly, it was "black, hearse-like, dignified, a rolling memento mori."[31]

Toward the end of 1958, O'Connor finally started making real progress on *The Violent Bear It Away*. On November 8 she wrote to Betty Hester that she was "heading toward the end" of the book. Around the same time, she found out she was making another kind of progress. Dr. Merrill announced that her hip-bone was recalcifying. He gave her permission to walk around the house without crutches for short periods of time. "They told me last year that I wouldn't get any better," she wrote to Father McCown. "I am willing to lay this to Lourdes or somebody's prayers but I hope the improvement will continue."

For all that, however, she was more desirous of the priest's prayers for her novel than for her bones. "I am at the most critical point in my novel," she wrote. "I would rather finish this novel right than be able to walk at all. It requires a lot more than I have."[32]

Katie Semmes died in late November. Only days earlier she had heard the news that the cousin she dragged to Lourdes had indeed experienced some of the healing that Katie had hoped so earnestly for.

11 | *THE VIOLENT BEAR IT AWAY:*
1959–1960

Soon after the start of 1959, O'Connor finally had a complete draft of *The Violent Bear It Away*. It had been six years since she started—six years of false starts and do-overs and hiatuses—and she still had a lot of work to do, but her rapid progress in the last few months of 1958 felt to O'Connor no less miraculous than the recalcification of her hip.

O'Connor bought herself a new typewriter and started re-typing a clean copy of *The Violent Bear It Away* to send to Caroline Gordon; as usual, she relied on her friend's critique before she was ready to send it on to her editor Robert Giroux. She also would send a copy to the Fitzgeralds, to Betty Hester, and to Catharine Carver who, though no longer her editor, was still a trusted literary advisor. O'Connor had been working on the book for so long that she was in no rush to send it to the editor now. "I am 100% pure sick of the sight of it," she told Carver, "but having been with it this long, I can stay with it some more."[1]

She had other things to do, however, than to stew over *The Violent Bear It Away*. In February she spent almost a week at the University of Chicago as a visiting writer—a late replacement for Eudora Welty. It was not a red-letter week. In the run-up to her trip, she wrote of her apprehensions about the "city inter-leckchuls" and the perils of traveling into a Chicago winter. She had little to fear from the interleckchuls, against whom she could hold her own, but the travel and the weather were legitimate concerns for a woman on aluminum crutches traveling alone.

O'Connor made a game of regaling her correspondents with stories of her minor personal disasters (though, as a rule, she steered clear of her major personal disasters). Her trip to Chicago provided her with ample material. February is not an ideal time for a Georgia resident to visit Chicago in any case, but the weather was more "revolting" than usual. A snowstorm grounded her plane in Louisville; she took a bus the rest of the way to Chicago, arriving at two in the morning bleary-eyed and haggard.

Though she was a literary star, in Chicago O'Connor was subjected to the small humiliations that writers endure whenever they venture into the wider world. She gave a public reading, but, as she told Betty Hester, "there was no public." To the few people who showed up, she read "A Good Man Is Hard to Find," which had become her standby for public readings. Self-conscious about taking the stage in front of a Northern audience, she chose to omit the paragraph "about the little nigger who doesn't have any britches on." As she told Betty Hester, "I can write with ease what I forbear to read."[2]

Besides the public reading, O'Connor also presided at two writing seminars, though "they didn't have much in the way of writing students." But the most galling part of her visit to Chicago was the fact that she was required to stay in the dormitory for five days and interact with the undergraduates. As she told her friend Elizabeth Bishop, "Some old lady left them money to have a woman-writer or some other female character live in the dormitory a week and be asked questions." The questions, rather than closing the gap between O'Connor and her interlocutors, only widened the chasm: "The low point was reached when—after a good ten-minute silence—one little girl said, 'Miss O'Connor, what are the Christmas customs in Georgia?'"[3]

Her feelings were no doubt soothed, however, by news she received the same week: she had been awarded an $8,000 grant from the Ford Foundation. To put the money in context, the $700 she got for her week in Chicago was the largest fee she had ever collected for a speaking engagement. She had never been paid more than $425 for a short story. The purpose of the grant was to keep her from having to make such reading and lecture tours for two years, allowing her to focus on her fiction. "But I don't *ever* want to work," she wrote to her friend Thomas Stritch, "so it's up to me to multiply the talent." A few years earlier she had invested her $2,000 from the Kenyon Fellowship in a rental property that was still generating income—a house that was "subject to termites and poor white trash."[4] She did splurge on a new writing chair, but unaccustomed to "living like a Ford," she meant to stretch out the money over eight or ten years at least.

Later that spring she read and spoke at Vanderbilt University. She told Cecil Dawkins that she was thinking about reading "The Artificial Nigger." "I won't be hurting anybody's feelings," she said, recalling the unease she felt when reading in Chicago. "It is great to be at home in a region," she said, "even this one."[5] O'Connor's views on region and race were complex, but this last sentiment is as good a one-sentence summary as any. Never proud of the South's racial past (or present), neither was she willing to concede that race relations in any other region were much better. She delighted in a story that Brainard Cheney told her that spring: he had gone to New York to do research for a novel about interracial friendships, but after two weeks of trying, his "liberal abolishionist friends" never managed to introduce him to a single black person socially. O'Connor couldn't help gloating: "Well, at least down here we are benighted over the table not under it."[6]

Even if she felt at home in Nashville and liked the "very nice atmosphere" of Vanderbilt's English Department, O'Connor could never quite feel at ease in academic settings. On her return from Vanderbilt she wrote, "I . . . have had enough of writers for a while, black or white. Whoever invented the cocktail party should have been drawn and quartered."[7] She was bothered by the academic tendency to treat stories as problems or puzzles to be worked out. "In most English classes the short story has become a kind of literary specimen to be dissected. Every time a story of mine appears in a Freshman anthology, I have a vision of it, with its little organs laid open, like a frog in a bottle."[8]

O'Connor had little patience for the sort of questions that students and teachers asked about her stories. She wrote of a young teacher at Macon's Wesleyan College, "an earnest type," who asked all the wrong questions after a reading of "A Good Man Is Hard to Find":

> "Miss O'Connor," he said, "why was the Misfit's hat *black*?" I said most countrymen in Georgia wore black hats. He looked pretty disappointed. Then he said, "Miss O'Connor, the Misfit represents Christ, does he not?" "He does not," I said. He looked crushed. "Well, Miss O'Connor," he said, "what is the significance of the Misfit's hat?" I said it was to cover his head;

and after that he left me alone. Anyway, that's what's happening to the teaching of literature.[9]

Any euphoria O'Connor felt as she completed the draft of *The Violent Bear It Away* quickly gave way to the doubts that so often beset a writer. In the spring of 1959 she described herself as being in "that state of not knowing whether it works or is the worst novel ever written."[10] She told Betty Hester that she was "more and more satisfied with the title and less and less satisfied with the rest of it."[11] The best she could say of it was that "nobody else would have wanted to write it but me."[12] That was true enough. For better or worse, *The Violent Bear It Away* is O'Connor distilled and fortified.

The summary of the story that O'Connor sent to Elizabeth Bishop points to how much her second novel has in common with her first: "My book is about a boy who has been raised up in the backwoods by his great uncle to be a prophet. The book is about his struggle not to be a prophet—which he loses."[13] Francis Marion Tarwater is yet another Protestant prophet tormented by wise blood—that visceral hunger for the holy—that holds him accountable to truths he would rather not face.

From the first sentence, it is clear that O'Connor is painting a picture of the fallen world at its ugliest:

Francis Marion Tarwater's uncle had been dead for only half a day when the boy got too drunk to finish digging his grave and a Negro named Buford Munson, who had come to get a jug filled, had to finish it and drag the body from the breakfast table where it was still sitting and bury it in a decent and Christian way, with the sign of its Saviour at the head of the grave and enough dirt on top to keep the dogs from digging it up.[14]

The sign of the Savior juxtaposed with those sniffing dogs looking to uncover an old man's rotting flesh: Transcendence asserting itself in a world that, on its own momentum, runs forever to ruin. That one long opening sentence is O'Connor's body of work in a capsule.

It is an unusual training ground for a young prophet, this moonshiner's homestead in the backwoods. Our first glimpse of the prophet, fourteen years old and stumbling drunk, gives us little reason to believe he will lose his struggle not to be a prophet. When the devil himself shows up in chapter one, young Tarwater is eager enough to follow his lead. But the devil, as always, is doing the Father's work in spite of himself. As dark as it is, *The Violent Bear It Away* is a drama of redemption all the same. Tarwater's tenuous grasp of reality doesn't change the fact that ultimate realities have a firm grasp on him.

In March 1959, O'Connor started reworking the middle of *The Violent Bear It Away* on the advice of Caroline Tate. By July, she was ready to send the manuscript to the publisher, but even then doubts continued to assail her. Catharine Carver told her it was the best thing she had ever written, but O'Connor wasn't sure—and she certainly wasn't sure the reading public would think it was any good. "I dread all the reviews, all the misunderstanding of my intentions, etc. etc. Sometimes the most you can ask is to be ignored."[15]

O'Connor's chief concern was that her audience would be "so far de-Christianized" that they would be unable to understand the book at all. One of the book's main characters is Rayber, uncle to young Tarwater and nephew to old Tarwater. He is a schoolteacher and a thoroughly modern man, interested in the psychological roots of the Tarwaters' prophetic ravings, but never considering their spiritual import. "The modern reader will identify himself with the schoolteacher," O'Connor wrote to John Hawkes, "but it is the old man who speaks for me."[16] It is not hard to imagine old Tarwater—or young Tarwater either—fighting an angel, like little Mary Flannery shut in her room and having it out with her celestial guardian. The Tarwaters' vision, like O'Connor's, is terrible, but still it is a vision of mercy.

O'Connor's letters in the interval between the submission of the manuscript and the publication of *The Violent Bear It Away* suggest that she was gearing up to explain herself. Theological musings occur throughout *The Habit of Being*, but her letters from the second half of 1959 seem more concerned than usual with theological matters. She seemed especially interested in questions of spiritual authority on the one hand and mystery on the other.

O'Connor's stories are about people feeling their way toward grace—or fumbling blindly toward it, or perhaps running in vain away from it. The Protestant prophets are guided by "wise blood," a kind of instinct for the Ultimate.

> Wise blood has to be these people's means of grace—they have no sacraments. The religion of the South is a do-it-yourself religion, something which I as a Catholic find painful and touching and grimly comic. It's full of unconscious pride that lands them in all sorts of ridiculous religious predicaments. They have nothing to correct their practical heresies and so they work them out dramatically. If this were merely comic to me, it would be no good, but I accept the same fundamental doctrines of sin and redemption and judgment that they do.[17]

O'Connor shared fundamental doctrines with the Tarwaters and Hazel Motes and the tent-revival preachers who toured her native South. But she always saw herself as speaking with an authority that was not her own. She submitted herself to it without always understanding agreeing; a belief, in O'Connor's understanding of things, was something to be *received*, not figured out. "The good Catholic acts upon the beliefs (assumptions if you want to call them that) that he receives from the Church.... If you want to know what Catholic belief is you will have to study what the Church teaches in matters of faith and morals."[18]

Sin and grace and forgiveness and love and mercy and hell and heaven are all mysteries. "If they were such that we could understand them, they wouldn't be worth understanding," O'Connor wrote. "A God you understood would be less than yourself."[19] For O'Connor, the purpose of fiction was to portray these and other mysteries—to embody them—in human manners. She did not expect fiction to explain mystery, but to gesture at its unfathomable depths, and thus to preserve the mystery that dogma guards. "Dogma is the guardian of mystery," she wrote. "The doctrines are spiritually significant in ways that we cannot fathom."[20]

The role of the prophet and the role of the fiction writer overlap, in O'Connor's view, in that the imagination is the conduit for both. This view she derived, not surprisingly, from Thomas Aquinas.

The Church's vision is prophetic vision; it is always widening the view. The ordinary person does not have prophetic vision but he can accept it on faith. St. Thomas also says that prophetic vision is a quality of the imagination, that it does not have anything to do with the moral life of the prophet. It is the imaginative vision itself that endorses the morality. The Church stands for and preserves always what is larger than human understanding.[21]

O'Connor's apprehensions about *The Violent Bear It Away* continued as the February 1960 publication day approached. She wrote to Betty Hester, "I am not afraid that the book will be controversial, I'm afraid it will not be controversial. I'm afraid it will just be dammed and dropped, genteelly sneered at, a few superior kicks from one or two and that will be that." She was uncharacteristically—and preemptively—defensive on the subject of young Tarwater three months before the novel was published:

> I don't feel Tarwater is such a monster. I feel that in his place I would have done everything he did. Tarwater is made up out of my saying: what would I do here? I don't think he's a caricature. I find him entirely believable, plausible, given his circumstances. Well, we will have to wait and see. I expect the worst. At least this is an individual book. I can't think of anybody else's that it will remind you of. Nobody would have been found dead writing it but me.[22]

Advance copies of the novel went out around the New Year, and in January 1960, early reviews began to trickle in. O'Connor's fears, as it turned out, were based in reality. *Library Journal*'s review described O'Connor as being "compelled more by a moral need than as an artist" and dismissed Tarwater as just another member of O'Connor's "band of poor God-driven Southern whites." (In the eyes of literary critics, O'Connor quipped, God-drivenness is "a form of Southern degeneracy."[23])

O'Connor was cheered, however, by encouraging words from Andrew Lytle, who had read an advance copy. "There are not many people whose opinion on this I set store by," she told Lytle, but he was one of them. She wrote to him, "I have got to the point now where I keep thinking more and more about the presentation of love and charity, or better call it grace, as love suggests tenderness, whereas grace can be violent or would have to be to compete with the kind of evil I can make concrete."[24]

The critics—even the critics who spoke approvingly of *The Violent Bear It Away*—for the most part lacked the theological equipment to understand what O'Connor was doing, even though she telegraphed her intentions in the title. The astonishing violence of the novel—verbal, symbolic, and physical—is a means of grace, the means by which the kingdom of God is seized. These aren't tender mercies O'Connor speaks of. She seems to have heeded the same call to which young Tarwater finally submits: "GO WARN THE CHILDREN OF GOD OF THE TERRIBLE SPEED OF MERCY." [25]

The review that most infuriated O'Connor appeared in *Time* magazine under the title "God-Intoxicated Hillbillies." *The Violent Bear It Away*, the reviewer wrote, is "a kind of horror story of faith.... While her handling of God-drunk backwoodsmen is based in religious seriousness, it seldom seems to rise above an ironic jape. It is this suggestion of the secure believer poking bitter fun at the confused and bedeviled that lingers in the mind after the tale is ended."[26]

O'Connor expected to be misunderstood. What she found inexcusable was the fact that the *Time* review made reference to her lupus. "*Time* can't hurt me," she wrote to Maryat Lee, "but I don't want further attention called to myself in this way. My lupus has no business in literary considerations."[27]

The *New Republic* described *The Violent Bear It Away*, for all its insight and scattered brilliance, as leaving a final impression of "crankiness and provincialism." As with *Wise Blood*, *The Violent Bear It Away*'s positive reviews, in O'Connor's view, didn't demonstrate real understanding of the book any better than the negative reviews. "It is to them all a trip in a glass-bottomed boat," she wrote.[28]

⚜

Shortly after the release of *The Violent Bear It Away*, O'Connor received a letter from a nun in Atlanta she had never met. Sister Evangelist, who served as Sister Superior of Our Lady of Perpetual Help Free Cancer Home, wrote to ask if O'Connor would be willing to help write the story of a little girl named Mary Ann who had lived in the Cancer Home from the age of three until she died at the age of twelve. "Of those nine years, much is to be told," wrote Sister Evangelist.

> Patients, visitors, Sisters, all were influenced in some way by this afflicted child. Yet one never thought of her as afflicted. True she had been born with a tumor on the side of her face; one eye had been removed, but the other eye sparkled, twinkled, danced mischievously, and after one meeting one never was conscious of her physical defect but recognized only the beautiful brave spirit and felt the joy of such contact.[29]

Sister Evangelist suggested that O'Connor might want to write a novelized version of Mary Ann's life.

O'Connor recoiled from the thought of writing a pious story of a pious little girl. Years before, she had spoken disparagingly of "baby stories and nun stories and little-girl stories." It almost seemed a divine joke that she was being invited to write the heartwarming story of a baby who grew into a little girl surrounded by nuns.

But when she looked at the picture of Mary Ann that Sister

Evangelist enclosed with her letter, she found herself strangely drawn to the little girl's deformed image:

> Her small face was straight and bright on one side. The other side was protuberant, the eye was bandaged, the nose and mouth crowded slightly out of place. The child looked out at her observer with an obvious happiness and composure. I continued to gaze at the picture long after I had thought to be finished with it.[30]

Nevertheless, O'Connor knew where her gifts lay, and they did not lie in the direction of inspirational stories about heroic children. She wrote to the Sisters saying that Mary Ann's story would need to be told as fact rather than fiction, and that the Sisters themselves were in the best possible position to report the facts. She did offer to help prepare the manuscript and do some light editing after the Sisters completed the writing. O'Connor believed that she had thereby extricated herself from the matter; by putting most of the work back on the nuns, she believed she had effectively killed the project. Nun-nurses in a cancer ward are busy people, after all.

In August, however, Sister Evangelist sent O'Connor a completed manuscript. Not surprisingly, the story of Mary Ann was not especially well told. Nevertheless, O'Connor was captured by the little girl's story. Deformed and dying from the first day the Sisters laid eyes on her, Mary Ann brought beauty and life to everyone who met her. The nuns, in turn, stoked the life in her even as they helped her prepare for her inevitable death. As O'Connor beautifully phrased it, "she fell into the hands of women who were shocked at nothing and who love life so much that they spend their own lives making comfortable those who have been pronounced incurable of cancer." Healthy children "were brought to the Home to visit her and were perhaps told when they left to think how thankful they should be that God had made their faces straight. It is doubtful if any of them were as fortunate as Mary Ann."[31]

O'Connor made good on her commitment to help the nuns complete the manuscript. She also wrote an introduction, a meditation on the beauty and deformity that coexisted in the face of that little girl. It is perhaps O'Connor's best articulation of what the grotesque meant in her fiction and in her whole worldview.

We are familiar enough with the face of evil, O'Connor argued, in part because we so often see it grinning back at us from the mirror. When we look at evil, we expect to see grotesquerie. But what of good? What does the face of good look like?

> Few have stared at [good] long enough to accept the fact that its face too is grotesque, that in us the good is something under construction. The modes of evil usually receive worthy expression. The modes of good have to be satisfied with a cliché or a smoothing-down that will soften their real look. When we look into the face of good, we are liable to see a face like Mary Ann's, full of promise.[32]

The suffering of children, O'Connor pointed out, is frequently trotted out as evidence that God is not good. This implies that the tenderness we feel toward suffering children is proof that God, if he exists, is less loving than we are. But this false tenderness is a measure of our spiritual blindness.

> If other ages felt less, they saw more, even though they saw with the blind, prophetical, unsentimental eye of acceptance, which

is to say, of faith. In the absence of this faith now, we govern by tenderness. It is a tenderness which, long since cut off from the person of Christ, is wrapped in theory. When tenderness is detached from the source of tenderness, its logical outcome is terror.[33]

The grotesque, the ugly in O'Connor's fiction, is more than a marker of human wickedness. It is a marker of the human imperfection, the human weakness, of which wickedness is only one expression. Our brokenness is the medium in which divine grace works. It is a central fact that makes love so necessary and so difficult. Mary Ann's beautiful deformity serves as a reminder of how the mystery of divine mercy works itself out in this sin-cursed world: "This action by which charity grows invisibly among us, entwining the living and the dead, is called by the Church the Communion of Saints. It is a communion created upon human imperfection, created from what we make of our grotesque state."[34]

When the manuscript for *A Memoir of Mary Ann* was complete, O'Connor dutifully forwarded it to Robert Giroux with a less-than-optimistic cover letter. "If you think there is any possibility at all of its getting published anywhere, I might be able to get them to improve it," she wrote.[35] She bet the Sisters a pair of peafowl that the manuscript would never see the light of day.

12 | "EVERYTHING THAT RISES MUST CONVERGE": 1961–1963

Toward the end of 1960, Flannery O'Connor began to notice a misalignment in her jaw. X-rays revealed that it was disintegrating as her hip had been for the last few years. She and her doctors realized that it was time to assess the state of her bones in general; she was admitted into Piedmont Hospital on December 12 for a battery of tests.

She was in the hospital for over a week getting X-rays and blood work. As always, she was quick to see the humor in her grim situation. She wrote to Maryat Lee of the woman in admitting— "who had carrot-colored hair and glasses to match"—asking the standard questions:

> "What's your bidnis?" she says. "I'm a writer," I says. She stopped typing & after a second said, "What?"
>
> "Writer," I says.
>
> She looked at me for a while, then she says, "How do you spell that?"[1]

O'Connor got home just before Christmas. Dr. Merrill determined that the bone disintegration was being caused by the corticosteroids that had been controlling the lupus for ten years. Merrill decided to discontinue the steroids and see how O'Connor's body reacted.

In January, she was surprised to learn from Robert Giroux that Farrar, Straus had indeed accepted *A Memoir of Mary Ann.* "The Sisters are dancing jigs up & down the halls," she wrote to Giroux.[2] True to her word, she sent a pair of peafowl to Our Lady of Perpetual Help Free Cancer Home. The Sisters had a seventy-five-foot run built for the birds, and they became favorites of the children in the home.

In return, the nuns sent O'Connor a small television. O'Connor told Brainard Cheney that she only watched the news and President Kennedy's press conferences, but as time went on the television became a means by which O'Connor furthered her researches into the ways of the vulgar. To one friend she admitted that she particularly liked the commercials. "My favorite is the one for Tube Rose Snuff," she said. "There is one for The Loan Arranger which Regina cannot see without comment."[3] She also got interested in stock-car racing (though she complained that on television "you don't see anything but cars"[4]) and watched the local sportscast every day. A fan of W. C. Fields, she watched his movies when they were on, begrudging the parts in which Fields himself was not on screen. "I think I might have written a picture that would be good for him," she said. "But it would be all him."[5]

After Dr. Merrill discontinued the steroids, O'Connor gave up traveling for the spring, assuming a wait-and-see posture. "I intend to sit quietly and write me some stories," she wrote. She considered buying an electric typewriter to save energy; at that time she was still pounding out her prose on an old manual machine.

The stories she was pounding out that winter and spring were "Parker's Back" and "Everything That Rises Must Converge." The Parker of "Parker's Back" is a man obsessed with tattoos. O'Connor was not much given to writing fiction *about* the power of art, choosing instead to create powerful art that spoke for itself. "Parker's Back" is an exception. And yet it is characteristically O'Connor: in one of the few passages in which a character finds his life changed by art, the art in question is the tattooed body of a sideshow performer. A fourteen-year-old Parker is transfixed by the bright, rippling mosaic of the tattooed man:

> Parker was filled with emotion, lifted up as some people are when the flag passes. . . . When the show was over, he had remained standing on the bench, staring where the tattooed man had been, until the tent was almost empty.
>
> Parker had never before felt the least motion of wonder in himself. Until he saw the man at the fair, it did not enter his head that there was anything out of the ordinary about the fact that he existed.[6]

The previously aimless Parker thus acquires a purpose, misguided as it may be. In a remarkable picture of self-worship, he sets about covering every inch of his body with tattoos, finally becoming his own religious icon when he has a huge Byzantine Christ inked onto his back, the last remaining real estate on his body.

O'Connor started "Parker's Back" in January 1961, but she finished it on her deathbed three and a half years later. "'Parker's Back' is not coming along too well," she complained. "It is too funny to be as serious as it ought."[7]

"Everything That Rises Must Converge," on the other hand, did come along well that spring. The story's title derives from Pierre Teilhard de Chardin, a Jesuit priest and paleontologist whose views on evolution got him in trouble with his church superiors. Teilhard viewed creation as an ongoing development. Evolution, in his view, was not strictly a biological or even a scientific process, but a moral and spiritual process as well, by which all of human life is converging toward a point that he called Omega—a point he identified with Christ.

Teilhard, a progressive thinker, challenged many of the certainties that had governed O'Connor's life—especially in the political, social, and racial realms. Nevertheless, she was energized by his work. "He was alive to everything there was to be alive to," she wrote.[8]

In "Everything That Rises Must Converge," O'Connor sought to apply Teilhard's idea of convergence "to a certain situation in the Southern states & indeed in all the world."[9] The story mostly takes place on a city bus, that crucible of racial politics in the American South of the 1950s and '60s. The typical dyad of the overbearing mother and her liberal adult son is joined by the mother's black doppelgänger—a personification of the convergence that will inevitably result from the rising fortunes of African Americans. The white characters—the progressive no less than the reactionary—find that they are ill-prepared for such a convergence.

O'Connor called the story "my reflection on the race situation." Indeed, though race figures into most of her stories one way or another, "Everything That Rises" is the only story that so consciously and directly addresses the changing dynamics of race in the South as a "situation." Even so, "Everything That Rises" is still a story about interpersonal, familial relationships more than it is a story about race. The atmosphere of the story is racially charged; nevertheless, the most important drama that plays out in that atmosphere plays out between the mother and the son. When the young man enters into "the world of guilt and sorrow," his guilt is over his sins against his mother, not over his sins against the black woman on the bus or black people generally. Perhaps O'Connor's "reflection on the race situation" is that even as the races rise and converge, we are still accountable to one another as individuals, not as races. As deep as the "race problem" goes, it is still not our deepest problem; it is one of the most obvious symptoms of our deeper problem of sin.

In April 1961, O'Connor had cortisone and novocaine injections in both hips, but the relief that the shots offered only lasted two weeks. When the pain returned, O'Connor started campaigning for a hip replacement operation. The orthopedic surgeon was willing to do it, but Dr. Merrill forbade it, fearing that the bodily stress of surgery would reignite the lupus that had been in a dormant phase. As he had told her when she was in the hospital before the previous Christmas, "it is better to be alive with joint trouble than dead without it."[10] She would have to live with the pain—with what Teilhard called "passive diminishment."

In July 1961, Caroline Gordon paid the O'Connor women a visit at Andalusia. She read an early draft of "The Lame Shall Enter First" and gave harsher criticism than O'Connor had been accustomed to. She pointed out "how it was completely undramatic and a million other things that I could have seen myself if I had had the energy." Ever the artist, ever striving to get better at her art, O'Connor took her friend's criticism to heart: "So much of my problem is laziness, not physical laziness so much as mental, not taking the trouble to think how a thing ought to be dramatized. I have written so many stories without thinking that when I have to think about one, it is painful."[11]

Gordon feared that O'Connor's dramatic sense had been compromised by all the speeches and essays she had been writing. O'Connor resolved to kick the nonfiction habit and again devote herself fully to fiction (and letters). But her artistic troubles seemed to go deeper than that. She was entering a dry spell that would last, with a couple of blessed interruptions, to the end of the short time she had remaining.

As the summer of 1961 progressed, good news continued to come in for *A Memoir of Mary Ann.* In July, *Good Housekeeping* magazine paid $4,500 to feature it in the Christmas issue. O'Connor's $1,125 share of that amount was the most she had ever been paid for a story (her previous record was $750 for "The King of the Birds," a piece about peacocks published that same summer in *Holiday* magazine). Also in July, Burnes & Oates of London bought the British rights to Mary Ann's story. O'Connor remarked, "It is almost comical how speedily it is proceeding, this project of the Lord's. I feel it is that."[12]

In October 1961, Betty Hester wrote to O'Connor to tell her that she was leaving the Church only five years after entering it. She told O'Connor that self-hatred had always caused her to try to be someone else; her Christian phase, she had come to believe, was just another effort to be someone she was not. But now, thanks in part to her experience in the church, she felt free to be herself— and free to leave the church.

"I don't know anything that could grieve us here like this news," O'Connor wrote to her friend. She reassured Hester that she was still her friend, but she was pained by "the realization that this means a narrowing of life for you and a lessening of the desire for life. . . . The loss of [faith] is basically a failure of appetite, assisted by sterile intellect."[13]

In her letters immediately after Hester's un-conversion, O'Connor is even clearer than usual in her articulation of the nature of her faith. "Faith comes and goes," she wrote. "It rises and falls like the tides of an invisible ocean. If it is presumptuous to think that faith will stay with you forever, it is just as presumptuous to think that unbelief will."[14]

Faith, in O'Connor's view, involves a self-forgetfulness, the heart of which is not self-abnegation, but rather a release from the tyranny of self-regard.

> I am glad the Church has given you the ability to look at yourself and like yourself as you are. The natural comes before the supernatural and that is perhaps the first step toward finding the Church again. Then you will wonder why it was necessary to look at yourself or like or dislike yourself at all. You will have found Christ when you are concerned with other people's sufferings and not your own.[15]

In a later letter, O'Connor's tone is more direct and not quite as tender: "What I do wonder at is that you were in the Church five years and came out with such a poor understanding of what the Church teaches—that you confuse self-abandonment in the Christian sense with a refusal to be yourself, with self-torture. . . . Self-torture is abnormal; asceticism is not."[16]

For O'Connor, that self-abandonment was not only a spiritual matter, but also an artistic matter. The self-forgetfulness of the artist, like the self-forgetfulness of the Christian, is the path toward fulfillment. He who loses his life shall find it. It is one of the great paradoxes of the faith.

> Writing is a good example of self-abandonment. I never completely forget myself except when I am writing and I am never more completely myself than when I am writing. It is the same with Christian self-abandonment. The great difference between Christianity and the Eastern religions is the Christian insistence on the fulfillment of the individual person.[17]

Hester never returned to the church. Yet she and O'Connor never slackened in their correspondence, and the letters were as friendly as ever. But the theological intensity of their first six years of correspondence flamed out with those letters O'Connor wrote immediately after Hester left the church.

In the fall of 1961, O'Connor circled back around to "The Lame Shall Enter First," the story that Caroline Gordon criticized as undramatic. O'Connor described it in that early stage as "a composite of all the eccentricities of my writing," and feared it would come across as some sort of self-parody—not an unfounded fear. The story orbits around a clubfooted juvenile delinquent named Rufus Johnson, "one of Tarwater's terrible cousins." He outmaneuvers a well-meaning, misguided social worker named Sheppard—"a man who thought he was good and thought he was doing good when he wasn't. . . . If Sheppard represents anything here," O'Connor wrote to her friend Cecil Dawkins, "it is, as he realizes at the end of the story, the empty man who fills up his emptiness with good works."[18]

O'Connor struggled with "The Lame Shall Enter First" for many months after Caroline Gordon gave her sharp critique, never quite able to get it to suit her. Andrew Lytle, however, had accepted the story for the summer issue of the *Sewanee Review*, an issue which would also include several critical essays on her work. In the face of that deadline, she told Betty Hester, "I'll just keep on sweating, I guess."

O'Connor was at a point where all of her writing required a lot of sweating. In March 1962 she wrote to Father McCown, "Pray that the Lord will send me some more [stories]. I've been writing for sixteen years and I have the sense of having exhausted my original potentiality and being now in need of the kind of grace that deepens perception, a new shot of life or something."[19] In fact, she wrote no new stories in 1962.

Instead, she traveled and gave talks and readings, in spite of her earlier assurances to Caroline Gordon. In the spring she went to North Carolina State University and Meredith College, a women's college also in Raleigh, North Carolina, then to Converse College in Spartanburg, South Carolina, where she participated in a literary festival with Eudora Welty, Cleanth Brooks, and Andrew Lytle. The next week, she traveled to Rosary College in Chicago, then Notre Dame, "then home with my tongue hanging out and a firm resolve not to go anywhere else for as long as possible."[20]

In the summer O'Connor took the first steps toward a third novel. She envisioned it as an expansion of "The Enduring Chill," the story of the struggling young writer who comes back from New York City to die on the family farm, only to learn that he is not dying, merely debilitated. She called it "Why Do the Heathen Rage?" Progress was slow—though no more so than on the two novels she successfully completed.

In the fall she started up the tour again, visiting colleges in Louisana and Texas, where she fielded such questions as "What is your motivation in writing?" (Answer: "Because I am good at it.") She also made her first visit to New Orleans, where she spoke at three colleges and met the novelist Walker Percy, who had just won the National Book Award for *The Moviegoer*. An old friend from Milledgeville was curator of the Jazz Museum at Tulane, and he showed her around the city. New Orleans made a favorable impression on her. She told John Hawkes, "If I had to live in a city I think I would prefer New Orleans to any other—both Southern and Catholic and with indications that the Devil's existence is freely recognized."[21]

As 1962 gave way to 1963, O'Connor's writer's block continued unabated. She laid aside "Why Do the Heathen Rage?" but was unable to write much else, other than a talk to be delivered at Sweetbriar College and a new, one-paragraph foreword to *Wise Blood* that Giroux required of her before Farrar, Straus could reissue the novel, which had originally been published by Harcourt, Brace. She used this short foreword to strike back at the critics who had so misunderstood both of her novels and her short stories:

> That belief in Christ is to some a matter of life and death has been a stumbling block for readers who would prefer to think it a matter of no great consequence. For them Hazel Motes' integrity lies in his trying with such vigor to get rid of the ragged figure who moves from tree to tree in the back of his mind. For the author Hazel's integrity lies in his not being able to. . . . Freedom cannot be conceived simply. It is a mystery and one which a novel, even a comic novel, can only be asked to deepen. [22]

Her experience at Sweetbriar—at the Symposium on Religion and Art—was overshadowed by the same concerns that shaped her foreword to *Wise Blood*. On returning she wrote to the Fitzgeralds, "boy do I have a stomach full of liberal religion!" She described a talk she heard on art and magic, the gist of which was that "religion was good because it was art and magic. Nothing behind it but it's good for you." After a number of talks about symbology, she said, "I waded in and gave them a nasty dose of orthodoxy, which I am sure they thought was pretty quaint."[23]

O'Connor continued her college tour, visiting Troy State and the University of Georgia after Sweetbriar in the spring of 1963. The fiction drought dragged on. She worked on "Why Do the Heathen Rage?" but the pages she produced remained a disjointed mess. After "working all summer just like a squirril on a treadmill" she was almost ready to conclude that "this is maybe not my material."[24]

Some writers' failure to produce, she told her friend Tom Stritch, results from a defect of patience. In her case, she had plenty of patience, but a defect of energy. She had been battling a shortage of physical energy for more than thirteen years, but it seemed that she was starting to lose the battle. To Sister Mariella Gable, a nun she met on one of her visits to St. Louis, she wrote, "I appreciate and need your prayers. I've been writing eighteen years and I've reached the point where I can't do again what I know I can do well, and the larger things that I need to do now I doubt my capacity for doing."[25]

Toward the end of the summer, O'Connor got a diagnosis that helped explain the low energy that had deviled her on top of her joint trouble and her lupus. Blood tests showed that she was anemic. She started taking iron, which seemed to help. Between travels in the fall, she knocked out the story "Revelation" in eight weeks. At the end of November she announced to Maryat Lee, "I have writ a story with which I am, for the time anyway, pleased, pleased, pleased."[26] To Betty Hester she wrote, "It was one of those rare ones in which every gesture gave me great pleasure in the writing."[27]

Half of "Revelation" is set in a doctor's waiting room—a setting O'Connor had had ample opportunity to observe. While waiting for the doctor to examine an ulcerated sore on her husband Claud's leg, Ruby Turpin is attacked by a terrifying, purple-faced Wellesley student named Mary Grace, whose hostility causes Mrs. Turpin to confront her own spiritual condition. The chatter in the waiting room is pitch-perfect, as if O'Connor had been taking notes all those hours she had sat and waited. Indeed, she told a friend that the story "was my reward for setting in the doctor's office. Mrs. Turpin I found there last fall. Mary Grace I found in my head, doubtless as a result of reading too much theology."[28]

The story that begins with the banality of a doctor's waiting room ends with a glorious vision of all the saints marching toward heaven across a purpled sky. Lifted out of her pettiness, Mrs. Turpin hears "the voices of the souls climbing upward into the starry field and shouting hallelujah."[29] Flannery O'Connor had less than a year to live when she wrote those words—less than a year before she would hear for herself the hallelujahs sung by the blessed.

13 | "BEYOND THE REGIONS OF THUNDER": 1964

One night shortly before Christmas 1963, Flannery O'Connor fainted. "Not enough blood to run the engine or something,"[1] she explained to Betty Hester. She spent the next ten days in bed. She was so weak, in fact, that she stayed home rather than attending Christmas Mass.

By New Year's Eve she was able to get out of bed for brief spells, but every movement tired her out. She lacked even the energy to pound out letters on her manual typewriter. When she got out of bed, her instructions were "to just creep around" while her blood count crept toward normal. By January 25, O'Connor declared herself "fully restored"—a diagnosis that would prove to be altogether too hasty.

For at least a year O'Connor and Giroux had kicked around the idea of putting together a second short story collection to be called *Everything That Rises Must Converge*. But O'Connor had been in no hurry. The previous January she had told Elizabeth McKee that she had enough stories to make a collection, but she wasn't yet ready to think about gathering them into a single volume.

After her fainting spell, however, O'Connor suddenly *was* ready to think about the new anthology of stories. Though she tended to downplay her illness in her letters, her new diligence about completing *Everything That Rises Must Converge* in a timely manner suggests that she might have had some idea that her time was short. "Revelation" made eight stories for the collection, she told Giroux, and she was still working on "Parker's Back," though she still wasn't sure whether the story would turn out or not.

In February, O'Connor's doctors determined that her anemia was being caused by a large fibroid tumor, for which the usual treatment was a hysterectomy. In the past, Dr. Merrill had been insistent that O'Connor not undergo surgery for fear that the bodily trauma would reignite the lupus that had lain dormant so many years. But it was apparent that she would not be able to function without such an operation.

The surgery was scheduled for February 25. O'Connor joked, "If they don't make haste and get rid of [the tumor], they will have to remove me and leave it."[2] She canceled all her travel plans. Because her aunt was hospitalized in the local hospital, O'Connor insisted on having the surgery performed in Milledgeville rather than traveling to Piedmont Hospital in Atlanta; she didn't want her mother to be torn between caring for her and caring for her aunt.

After the surgery, she was typically positive. "It was all a howling success from [the surgeons'] point of view and one of them is going to write it up for a doctor magazine as you usually don't cut folks with lupus."[3] Janet McKane, a schoolteacher in New York City who had recently become one of O'Connor's most important pen pals, had a high Mass said for her in a Byzantine rite church. Another, less tasteful tribute came from some nuns in Canada: "A Check on the Bank of Heaven," which read, "'Pay to the order of *Flannery O'Connor* 300 Hail Marys.' At one corner is a picture of the Christ Child, & under this the word *President*. On the other side is the Virgin—*Vice-President!* It takes a strong faith and a stronger stomach," O'Connor remarked.[4]

O'Connor's recovery from the surgery seemed at first to be on track. She suffered some bladder trouble and a kidney infection, but she considered those side effects of the hysterectomy. By the time a month had passed, however, she began to suspect that the surgery had reactivated her lupus. The infection she had downplayed a week before had gotten worse, and she was back on steroids.

By the beginning of April 1964, O'Connor's health was getting worse. The kidney infection had outlasted five different antibiotics. "None have done anything to the infection though they have done several things to me—torn up my stomach and swollen shut my eyes. Then the cortisone comes along and undoes the swollen eyes but gives you a moon-like face."[5] Now back on steroids indefinitely, O'Connor was looking forward to getting them regulated so she could go back to work. She joked to a friend in Chicago about her health: "It ain't much but I'm able to take nourishment and participate in a few Klan rallies."[6]

Dr. Merrill changed O'Connor's antibiotic one more time, and it finally conquered the kidney infection. It gave O'Connor hope, as did the miraculous recovery of her Aunt Mary, who had been in the hospital at the same time as Flannery. Regina had called the family to the hospital to say their good-byes. But Mary pulled through and was giving orders again just as she always had—sitting up in bed now rather than giving orders from a supine position. "This family is full of creakers," O'Connor told Maryat Lee. "We creak along to about the age of 96. Look for me to be this kind too. I feel a lot better."[7]

Just four days after writing that hopeful letter, however, O'Connor woke up covered with the lupus rash. It was the one major lupus symptom that she had never suffered before. That same day she went to Baldwin General for an indefinite stay—"the guest of myself," she said, "as my insurance don't cover lupus." She was in the hospital for two weeks that time. She wrote Elizabeth McKee from her hospital bed with specific instructions for the short stories she wanted to include in the *Everything That Rises* collection.

The plan had been for O'Connor to revise and rework the stories, most of which had appeared previously in magazines. But given her physical limitations, she suggested that her editors at Farrar instead obtain permissions from the magazines and print from those. "If I were well there is a lot of rewriting and polishing I could do, but in my present state of health I see no reason for me to spend my energies on old stories that are essentially all right as they are."[8] In her letter to McKee, O'Connor gives the impression that Giroux was rushing her in order to include the book in the fall catalogue. But she had been in the business long enough to know how often books get bumped from one catalogue to the next. The real urgency would have come from her side, not from Giroux's.

Flannery and Aunt Mary left the hospital on the same day, and both came back to the house at Andalusia—"Creaking Hill Nursing Home," as Flannery called it—to be cared for by Regina. She reported that she felt no pain, only weakness. Regular blood transfusions made it possible for her to work an hour or so every day.

In New York, Janet McKane had another Mass said for O'Connor's intentions—in other words, a Mass said in her behalf. O'Connor played both wittingly and faithfully on that Catholic term "intentions": "I don't know what my intentions are but I try to say that whatever suits the Lord suits me. So I reckon you might say my intentions are honorable anyway."[9]

It was also her intention to finish her short story collection in time for a fall release. She worked steadily on the stories that needed revising or completing. Her efforts were interrupted, however, by another trip to the hospital—this time to Piedmont in Atlanta—so that Dr. Merrill might resume responsibility for her care.

O'Connor stayed in Piedmont Hospital from May 21 through June 20. She continued writing letters from her hospital bed. A few days in, her correspondence began to take on a less cheerful tone. "I don't know if I'm making progress or if there's any to be made," she wrote to Maryat Lee. "Let's hope they are learning something anyhow."[10]

For the first couple of weeks she put off working on "Parker's Back," the story that still needed the most reworking. She wrote to Giroux saying that she would get on it as soon as she got back to her typewriter. Eventually, however, she gave up and started writing longhand from her hospital bed. She also asked Giroux to delay publication until the spring.

When Dr. Merrill finally discharged O'Connor on June 20, it was not because she was better, but because there was nothing left for him to do for her. He put her back in the care of her Milledgeville doctors.

The day before she left the hospital, O'Connor wrote a letter to Janet McKane in which she mentioned that she admired the poet Gerard Manley Hopkins—and especially the sonnet titled "Spring and Fall." It is a meditation on death and the transience of life, as well as the nature of sorrow, spoken to a girl named Margaret, whose first taste of grief comes with the dying of the autumn leaves:

Margaret, are you grieving
Over Goldengrove unleaving?
Leaves, like the things of man, you
With your fresh thoughts care for, can you?
Ah! as the heart grows older
It will come to such sights colder
By and by, nor spare a sigh
Though worlds of wanwood leafmeal lie;
And yet you will weep and know why.
Now no matter, child, the name:
Sorrow's springs are the same.
Nor mouth had, no nor mind, expressed
What héart héard of, ghóst guéssed:
It is the blight man was born for,
It is Margaret you mourn for.

It is a heartbreaking thing to think of Flannery O'Connor in that hospital room, out of medical options, not yet forty and heading home to die, scratching out those sorrowful words to a woman she had never met: *Margaret, are you grieving?*

♪♪

Back at Andalusia, O'Connor worked as best she could, sustained by blood transfusions. She wrote to Cecil Dawkins, "As far as I'm concerned, as long as I can get at that typewriter, I have enough [blood]."[11] Her kidneys had become the focal point of her ailments; their failure to process her blood made the transfusions necessary.

She finished "Judgement Day"—a reworking of her first published story, "The Geranium." In its original form, the story was a rather sentimental meditation on homesickness and the evils of Southern racism. It was now a meditation on death that makes conventional Southern attitudes about race seem ephemeral in comparison. O'Connor sent it to Giroux to take the place of "The Partridge Festival," a story she had grown to dislike.

Once home, O'Connor cycled through ups and downs. In her correspondence she mostly reported the good days, but in a letter to Maryat Lee on the subject of her adjusted dosages, she wrote, "So far as I can see the medicine and the disease run neck & neck to kill you."[12] More significantly, and more ominously, when a priest came to Andalusia to give her the Eucharist after so many weeks away from Mass (and no prospects for returning anytime soon) she asked him to give her the Sacrament of the Sick—the sacrament formerly known as Extreme Unction.

Flannery O'Connor lived another three weeks. On Wednesday, July 29, she fell ill and was taken by ambulance to Baldwin General. On Sunday, August 2, family and local friends were alerted that the end was near. O'Connor received the Eucharist that day in her hospital bed.

She lost consciousness that night, and shortly after midnight on Monday, August 3, 1964, her kidneys failed and she died. She was thirty-nine years old.

O'Connor's funeral was the next day—a low requiem funeral Mass at Sacred Heart Church. None of her out-of-town friends were there. Only local friends and family were there to see the red clay cover her casket. She was a Milledgevillian to the end.

Two weeks before she died, O'Connor wrote Janet McKane a letter in which she reproduced a prayer to Saint Raphael that she prayed every day:

O Raphael, lead us toward those we are waiting for, those who are waiting for us: Raphael, angel of happy meeting, lead us by the hand toward those that we are looking for. May all our movements be guided by your Light and transfigured with your joy.

Angel, guide of Tobias, lay the request we now address to you at the feet of Him on whose unveiled Face you are privileged to gaze. Lonely and tired, crushed by the separations and sorrows of life, we feel the need of calling you and of pleading for the protection of your wings, so that we may not be as strangers in the province of joy, all ignorant of the concerns of our country. Remember the weak, you who are strong, you whose home lies beyond the region of thunder, in a land that is always peaceful, always serene and bright with the resplendent glory of God.[13]

It is remarkable to think about this woman—who had made a name for herself with stories of earthly terror and grotesquerie—meditating every day on the province of joy, lest she be ignorant of the concerns of her true country. All that darkness was in the service of eternal brightness. All that violence was in the service of peace and serenity. The writer whose every story was a thunderclap took her place beyond the region of thunder.

NOTES

Introduction

1. *The Habit of Being*, 65.
2. Ibid., 291.
3. *Complete Stories*, 147.
4. *The Habit of Being*, 81.
5. Ibid., 10.
6. Ibid., 82.
7. *Mystery and Manners*, 151.
8. Ibid., 163.
9. Ibid., 34.
10. *Complete Stories*, 500.
11. Ibid., 507.
12. Ibid., 508–09.
13. "Come, Ye Sinners, Poor and Needy," Joseph Hart, 1759.

Chapter 1: The Girl Who Fought with Angels: Savannah, 1925–1939

1. *Mystery and Manners*, 84.
2. Jean Cash, *Flannery O'Connor: A Life*, 11.
3. Ibid., 16.
4. *The Habit of Being*, 146.
5. *Flannery: A Life of Flannery O'Connor*, 30. Gooch is quoting a "Biography" Flannery O'Connor wrote, which is collected in the GSCU library.

6. Cash, 17–18.

7. *Mystery and Manners*, 4, from the essay, "King of the Birds."

8. *A Life of Flannery O'Connor*, 39.

9. *Realist of Distances*, 67.

10. *The Habit of Being*, 98.

11. Ibid., 114.

12. *A Life of Flannery O'Connor*, 33–34.

13. *The Habit of Being*, 139.

14. Ibid., 90.

15. Ibid., 131–32.

16. Ibid., 111.

17. Ibid., 100.

18. *A Life of Flannery O'Connor*, 40–41.

19. *The Habit of Being*, 136–37.

20. Cash, 9.

21. *The Habit of Being*, 166.

22. Ibid., 168.

23. Ibid., 169.

Chapter 2: "Mostly she talked Flannery": Milledgeville, 1939–1945

1. *Mystery and Manners*, 127.

2. *The Habit of Being*, 249.

3. Ibid., 239.

4. Cash, 48, quoting from an interview by mail.

5. *The Peabody Palladium*, December 18, 1941.

6. *The Habit of Being*, 98.

7. Cash, 56.

8. *Cartoons of Flannery O'Connor*, 4.

9. *The Habit of Being*, 536.

10. Cash, 67.

Chapter 3: "I began to read everything at once": Iowa, 1945–1948

1. *The Habit of Being*, 422.

2. *The Complete Stories*, vii.

3. Ibid., viii.
4. Cash, 81.
5. *The Habit of Being*, 242.
6. Ibid., 98.
7. *A Life of Flannery O'Connor*, 124–25.
8. Cash, 82–83.
9. *The Life You Save May Be Your Own*, 149.
10. *A Life of Flannery O'Connor*, 141–42.
11. Cash, 87.
12. Ibid., 88.
13. *A Life of Flannery O'Connor*, 146.

Chapter 4: "The peculiarity . . . of the experience I write from": New York and Connecticut, 1948–1950

1. *Time*, September 5, 1938. Also in *Beautiful Shadow: A Life of Patricia Highsmith*.
2. *The Habit of Being*, 362.
3. Ibid., 364.
4. *Ibid.*, 487.
5. Ibid., 487.
6. Ibid., 204.
7. *Collected Works*, 1243.
8. *A Life of Flannery O'Connor*, 160.
9. *The Habit of Being*, 152.
10. Ibid., 152.
11. Ibid., 9.
12. Ibid., 10.
13. Ibid., 14.
14. See Ruth Price's biography, *The Lives of Agnes Smedley*, Oxford: UP (2005).
15. *The Life You Save May Be Your Own*, 174.
16. Cash, 114, quoting *New York Jew*, 204.
17. *The Habit of Being*, 152.
18. Ibid., 395.
19. *Everything That Rises Must Converge*, xiii.

20. *The Habit of Being*, 21.

21. Ibid., 161.

22. Ibid., 17.

23. Ibid., 20.

24. *Everything That Rises Must Converge*, xiii.

Chapter 5: "Sickness is a place": 1951–1952

1. *The Habit of Being*, 21–22.

2. Ibid., 163.

3. Ibid., 22.

4. Ibid., 40.

5. Ibid., 35, letter to Robert Lowell.

6. Ibid., 26.

7. Ibid., 117.

8. Ibid., 117–18.

9. Ibid., 27.

10. Ibid., 23.

11. Ibid., 198.

12. Ibid., 23.

13. Ibid., 24.

14. Ibid., 25.

15. *The Life You Save May Be Your Own*, 193.

16. Ibid.

17. Ibid., 26.

18. *A Life of Flannery O'Connor*, 6. Gooch is quoting from *The Letters of Robert Lowell* ed. Saskia Hamilton (NY: FS&G, 2005), 211.

19. *The Habit of Being*, 27.

20. Ibid., 24.

21. Ibid., 27.

22. Ibid., 28.

23. *The Life You Save May Be Your Own*, 195.

24. *The Habit of Being*, 29.

25. Ibid., 30.

26. Ibid., 31.

27. Ibid., 35.

28. Ibid., 33.
29. Ibid., 33.

Chapter 6: *Wise Blood*: 1952

1. *The Habit of Being*, 35.
2. *Collected Works*, 896.
3. *The Habit of Being*, 36.
4. Cash, 176. Brad Gooch, who interviewed a number of Milledgevillians, is also excellent on the subject of the locals' reaction to *Wise Blood*. See pp. 208–11.
5. *A Life of Flannery O'Connor*, 208.
6. *The Habit of Being*, 35.
7. Ibid., 139.
8. *Collected Works*, 901.
9. Ibid., 897.
10. *The Habit of Being*, 81.
11. *The Critical Response to Flannery O'Connor*, 21.
12. Ibid., 20.
13. Ibid., 21.
14. The reviewer in *The New Republic* remarked that "the few figures one can make out in [*Wise Blood*] show in a pallid light reflected mainly, I should say, from Faulkner and Carson McCullars." *The Critical Response to Flannery O'Connor*, 22.
15. "A Master Class," *Georgia Review*, 33:4 (1979), 831–32.
16. *The Habit of Being*, 37.
17. *A Life of Flannery O'Connor*, 215.
18. *The Habit of Being*, 39.
19. Ibid.
20. Ibid., 42.
21. Ibid., 41.
22. Ibid., 49.
23. *Mystery and Manners*, 5.
24. Ibid., 16.
25. Ibid., 6.
26. Ibid., 10.

Chapter 7: "I seem to attract the lunatic fringe": 1953–1954

1. *The Habit of Being*, 54.
2. Ibid., 65.
3. Ibid., 54.
4. Ibid., 54.
5. Ibid., 57.
6. Ibid., 94.
7. *The Correspondence of Flannery O'Connor and the Brainard Cheneys*, 10.
8. Ibid., 86.
9. Ibid., 82.
10. Ibid., 197. Originally in *Shenandoah*, 3 (Autumn 1952), 55–60.
11. *The Correspondence of Flannery O'Connor and the Brainard Cheneys*, 3.
12. Ibid., 4–5.
13. *The Habit of Being*, 85.
14. *Mystery and Manners*, 112.
15. *The Habit of Being*, 367.
16. Ibid., 58.
17. Mark Bosco, S. J. "Erik Langkjaer: The One Flannery 'Used to Go With,'" *Flannery O'Connor Review*, vol. 5, 46.
18. *The Habit of Being*, 30.
19. Ibid., 69.
20. Ibid., 339.
21. "A View of the Woods" has a young girl as a character, but it is told from the point of view of her grandfather.
22. *The Habit of Being*, 67.
23. Bosco, 45.
24. Ibid., 47.
25. Ibid., 48–49.
26. Ibid., 50.

Chapter 8: *A Good Man Is Hard to Find*: 1954–1955

1. *The Habit of Being*, 172.
2. Ibid., 140.

3. *Complete Stories*, 270.

4. Ibid., 78.

5. *A Life of Flannery O'Connor*, 253. Quote originally appeared in Sally Fitzgerald and Ralph C. Wood, "Letters to the Editor." *Flannery O'Connor Bulletin* 23 (1994–95): 175–183.

6. *The Habit of Being*, 74.

7. *Complete Stories*, 284.

8. Ibid., 291.

9. *The Habit of Being*, 75.

10. Ibid., 81.

11. Ibid., 80.

12. Ibid., 106.

13. Ibid., 81.

14. Ibid., 89.

15. Ibid., 341.

16. Ibid., 81.

17. Ibid.

18. *Conversations with Flannery O'Connor*, 8.

19. *The Habit of Being*, 85.

20. Ibid., 76–77.

21. Ibid., 74.

22. *Critical Essays on Flannery O'Connor*, 24. Originally published in *New York Times Book Review*, 12 June 1955: 5.

23. *The Critical Response to Flannery O'Connor*, 24–25. Originally published in *Time*, 6 June 1955: 114.

24. *The Habit of Being*, 89.

25. *The Critical Response to Flannery O'Connor*, 26. Originally published in *Kenyon Review* XVII (1955): 664–70.

26. *The Habit of Being*, 90.

27. *Mystery and Manners*, 117.

28. *The Habit of Being*, 82.

29. Ibid., 157.

30. *Mystery and Manners*, 145.

31. Ibid., 147–48.

Chapter 9: "The accurate naming of the things of God": 1955–1956

1. *The Habit of Being*, 90.
2. Ibid., 89.
3. Ibid., 152.
4. Ibid., 90.
5. Ibid., 92.
6. Ibid.
7. Ibid.
8. Ibid., 99–100.
9. Ibid., 126, 128.
10. Ibid., 128.
11. Ibid., 125.
12. Ibid., 148.
13. Ibid., 148.
14. *A Life of Flannery O'Connor*, 270. His source: an email from a doctor.
15. *The Habit of Being*, 116–17.
16. Ibid., 131.
17. Ibid., 154.
18. Ibid., 101.
19. Ibid., 155.
20. Ibid., 151.
21. Quoted in *A Life of Flannery O'Connor*, 341, from a letter from Maryat Lee to Robert Giroux.
22. *The Habit of Being*, 163.
23. Ibid., 169.
24. Ibid., 175.
25. This passage is from a transcript of an NPR story about the release of the Betty Hester letters at Emory University. The story aired May 12, 2007. http://www.npr.org/templates/ story/story.php?storyId=10154699. For a more detailed account of the development of the friendship between O'Connor and Hester after this revelation, see Ralph C. Wood's article "Sacramental Suffering: The Friendship of

Flannery O'Connor and Elizabeth Hester." *Modern Theology*
24:3 (2008): 387–411.

26. *The Habit of Being*, 191.
27. Ibid., 174.
28. Ibid., 205.
29. Ibid., 206.
30. Ibid., 208.

Chapter 10: "The society I feed on": 1957–1958

1. *Collected Works*, 1019.
2. *The Habit of Being*, 195.
3. Ibid., 201.
4. Ibid., 218.
5. Ibid., 329.
6. *Flannery O'Connor and the Christ-Haunted South*, 94.
7. Ibid., 97. O'Connor is mistaken in attributing this quotation to Peter. It was the father of the sick boy in Mark 9:24 who said "help my unbelief."
8. *The Habit of Being*, 224.
9. Ibid., 230.
10. Ibid., 302–03.
11. *Mystery and Manners*, 40.
12. Ibid., 44
13. *The Habit of Being*, 229.
14. Ibid., 232.
15. Ibid., 250.
16. Ibid., 259.
17. Ibid., 134.
19. Ibid., 258.
19. Ibid., 272.
20. Ibid., 268.
21. Ibid., 286.
22. Ibid., 282.
23. Ibid., 280.
24. Ibid., 286.
25. Ibid., 285.

26. Ibid., 280.

27. *Collected Works*, 1071.

28. *The Habit of Being*, 282.

29. Ibid., 284.

30. Ibid., 268–69.

31. Ibid., 294.

32. Ibid., 310.

Chapter 11: *The Violent Bear It Away:* 1959–1960

1. *The Habit of Being*, 323.

2. Ibid.

3. Ibid., 327.

4. Ibid., 325.

5. Ibid., 321.

6. Ibid., 330.

7. Ibid., 329.

8. *Mystery and Manners*, 108.

9. *The Habit of Being*, 334.

10. Ibid., 320.

11. Ibid., 317.

12. Ibid., 323.

13. Ibid., 344.

14. *Three by Flannery O'Connor*, 125.

15. *The Habit of Being*, 340.

16. Ibid., 350.

17. Ibid., 350.

18. Ibid., 345.

19. Ibid., 354.

20. Ibid., 365.

21. Ibid., 365.

22. Ibid., 358.

23. Ibid., 371.

24. Ibid., 373.

25. *Three by Flannery O'Connor*, 267.

26. *The Critical Response to Flannery O'Connor*, 45–46. Originally appeared in *Time* February 1960: 118–19.

27. *The Habit of Being*, 379–80.

28. Ibid., 376.

29. *Mystery and Manners*, 214.

30. Ibid., 215.

31. Ibid., 224.

32. Ibid., 226.

33. Ibid., 227.

34. Ibid., 228.

35. *The Habit of Being*, 421.

Chapter 12: "Everything That Rises Must Converge": 1961–1963

1. *The Habit of Being*, 423.

2. Ibid., 428.

3. Ibid., 443.

4. Ibid., 523.

5. Ibid., 513.

6. *Complete Stories*, 513.

7. Ibid., 427.

8. *The Habit of Being*, 449.

9. Ibid., 438.

10. Ibid., 423.

11. Ibid., 445.

12. Ibid., 445.

13. Ibid., 452.

14. Ibid., 452.

15. Ibid., 453.

16. Ibid., 457–58.

17. Ibid., 458.

18. Ibid., 490–91.

19. Ibid., 468.

20. Ibid., 471.

21. Ibid., 500.

22. *Three by Flannery O'Connor*, 2.

23. Ibid., 510–11.

24. Ibid., 537.

25. Ibid., 518.

26. Ibid., 551.

27. Ibid., 552.

28. Ibid., 579.

29. *Complete Stories*, 509.

Chapter 13: "Beyond the regions of thunder": 1964

1. *The Habit of Being*, 554.

2. Ibid., 567.

3. Ibid., 568.

4. Ibid., 569.

5. Ibid., 572.

6. Ibid., 573.

7. Ibid., 574.

8. Ibid., 575.

9. Ibid., 577.

10. Ibid., 582–83.

11. Ibid., 587.

12. Ibid., 590.

13. Ibid., 592–93.

ACKNOWLEDGMENTS

Flannery O'Connor suggested that her creativity was driven in part at least by the fact that she needed people and didn't get them. That hasn't been my experience. I have always had people, and plenty of them. Their presence, not their absence, has turned me in a creative direction. I don't think I would have the heart to keep entering that lonesome cave where writing happens if there weren't people just outside the entrance, always calling me back to the bright life of the world.

Friendship is one of the world's great creative forces. My writing life was transformed seven years ago when I met Andrew Peterson, a man whose writing spills out of a fullness and generosity of soul. He introduced me to an orbit of musicians, writers, preachers, and teachers whose commitment to truth and beauty is matched only by their commitment to friendship and mutual help. My colleagues at the Rabbit Room (www.rabbitroom.com) have been a source of constant encouragement these last few years. I have watched them struggle through the creative process, and I have seen the raft of beautiful work that has come out of it. There could be no better reminder that the struggle is worth it. And though the Rabbit Room is a virtual place, there is nothing virtual about the many Waffle House biscuits I have broken with Pete Peterson, Russ Ramsey, Thomas McKenzie, Eric Peters, Randall Goodgame, Josh Shive, and Andy Osenga. We are becoming what Wendell Berry calls a membership, for which I am thankful.

I am thankful for Joel Miller, who first suggested that I write this book, and to Heather Skelton and Kristen Parrish, who shepherded it through the editorial process. I am also grateful to Rhonda Lowry for her help with permissions and to Ralph C. Wood, who rescued me at the eleventh hour from errors that I wouldn't have wanted the world to see.

As always, I owe my wife Lou Alice more thanks than I could say. She scatters beauty everywhere she goes and is supportive in more ways than one person should have to be.

ABOUT THE AUTHOR

Jonathan Rogers is originally from Middle Georgia, not very far from Flannery O'Connor's Milledgeville. He received an undergraduate degree from Furman University and holds a PhD in seventeenth-century literature from Vanderbilt University. He is also a lifelong devotee of the vernacular storytelling traditions of the American South.

Jonathan's previous books include the Wilderking Trilogy—*The Bark of the Bog Owl*, *The Secret of the Swamp King*, and *The Way of the Wilderking*—as well as *The Charlatan's Boy*. He lives in Nashville, Tennessee, with his wife, Lou Alice, and their six children.

INDEX

violence to return characters to, 78
redemption, 60, 61, 134
region
    discussion of, 119–120
    O'Connor's views on, 131–132
rejection, of O'Connor by other students, 17
relationships, of mother and adult child, 63
religious authority, O'Connor's relation to, 8–9
religious mania, 39
religious outliers, O'Connor interest in, 93
rental property, 131
research, television for, 144
"Revelation" (O'Connor), xv–xvi, 153–154, 156
rheumatoid arthritis diagnosis, 42, 44
Rinehart, 41
Rinehart-Iowa Award, 29
"The River" (O'Connor), 67
Rockefellers, fellowship award, 67
Rome, 125
Rosary College, 151

S
Sacrament of the Sick, 161
sacraments, 105
Sacred Heart Catholic Church, x
Sacred Heart School, 10

St. John's Cathedral, mandatory children's Mass, 8
St. Joseph's Hospital, Flannery Memorial Wing, 3
St. Mary's Church (Iowa City), 23
St. Vincent's Grammar School for Girls, 3, 9
    nuns' rules, 8
Saratoga Springs. *See* Yaddo artist's colony in Saratoga Springs
Saturday Review, 52
Savannah, Georgia, 1
    vs. Milledgeville, 15–16
    O'Connor family move from, 11–12
Schlitz Playhouse, 112
school-age relationships, of Flannery, 4–5
seeing straight, O'Connor on, 105
Selby, John, xii, 36–38
    release document from, 41
self-abandonment, 149
Semmes, Katie, 3
    death, 127
    pilgrimage to Europe, 121–122
    reaction to *Wise Blood*, 58
    trip to Lourdes, 124–125
Semmes, Raphael, 3
"separate but equal," 116
Sessions, Billy, 126
Sewanee Review, 28, 29, 151

sexual mores of Yaddo, 33
Shenandoah Quarterly, *Wise Blood* review, 74–75
Sheppard (social worker), 150
Shiftlet, Mr., xi
short stories, 63, 87
    early vs. later, 28
    O'Connor reaction to questions on, 132
    plans for collection, 155–156, 158–159
    significance, 109
sickness, as place, 44
"The Significance of the Short Story" (speech), 109
Smedley, Agnes, 38
social awkwardness in school, 17
Soubirous, Bernadette, 122
Southern Gothic, critics' understanding of, 62
Southern writers, 119–120
speaking engagements, 92
Spectrum (GSCW yearbook), 20
Stafford, Jean, Lowell marriage to, 35
Stegner, Wallace, 120
Steinbeck, John, 34
steroids. *See* corticosteroids
Stevens family (dairyman's family), 81
strangers, letters from, 74

visible universe, and invisible, 105
vulgar, research on, 72

W

Warren, Robert Penn, 25, 76
  Understanding Fiction, 26
Waugh, Evelyn, 55
WAVES, arrival on campus as cartoon topic, 20
"Why Do the Heathen Rage?" (O'Connor), 151
Wickers, Hazel (in "The Train"), 27
"Wildcat" (O'Connor), 28
Wise Blood, ix
  author talks after, 59
  community response, 72
  "Enoch and the Gorilla," 34
  family need to be prepared for, 56
  final preparations for publication, 55
  finished draft, 48
  first copy, 56
  first draft, 42
  "The Heart of the Park," 33
  Milledgeville locals' reaction to, 58
  misunderstood by reviewers, 60–62
  new foreword for reissue, 152
  O'Connor on qualities of, 36
  and O'Connor's view of own future, 48
  "The Peeler," 33–34
  published, 57
  review, 74–75
  "A Stroke of Good Fortune," 34
  "The Train" as first chapter, 27–28
  uncertain publication status, 41
  work at Yaddo, 36
  work from hospital bed, 47
  writing at Yaddo, 33–34
"wise blood," 93
"Woman on the Stairs" (O'Connor), 77
Wood, Ralph C., 118
  Flannery O'Connor and the Christ-Haunted South, 119
"The World Is Almost Rotten" (O'Connor), 63
writer's block, 151–152, 153
writing habits, 25

Y

Yaddo artist's colony in Saratoga Springs, 30, 31–34
  parties, 33
  Wise Blood work at, 36
"You Can't Be Any Poorer than Dead" (O'Connor), 107